Applauding

the

Strugglers

Applauding

the

Strugglers

JIM McGUIGGAN

WORD PUBLISHING
Nelson Word Ltd
Milton Keynes, England

WORD AUSTRALIA
Kilsyth, Australia

NELSON WORD CANADA LTD
Vancouver, B.C., Canada

STRUIK CHRISTIAN BOOKS (PTY) LTD
Cape Town, South Africa

JOINT DISTRIBUTORS SINGAPORE–
ALBY COMMERCIAL ENTERPRISES LTD
and
CAMPUS CRUSADE ASIA LTD

PHILIPPINE CAMPUS CRUSADE FOR CHRIST
Quezon City, Philippines

CHRISTIAN MARKETING NEW ZEALAND LTD
Havelock North, New Zealand

JENSCO LTD
Hong Kong

SALVATION BOOK CENTRE
Malaysia

APPLAUDING THE STRUGGLERS

Contents

To my sister
Margaret (McGuiggan) Jaconette
whose light has shone all
these years—constant,
bright, soft.

Though for myself alone
I would not be ambitious in my wish,
To wish myself much better, yet for you
I would be trebled twenty times myself;
A thousand times more fair,
ten thousand times more rich;
That, only to stand high in your account,
I might in virtues, beauties, livings, friends, exceed
account.

Shakespeare

Introduction

Mark Rutherford said he wanted to add a Beatitude:

Blessed is the one who gives us back our self-respect.

I've met a few in my life who were pleased with the fact that they were free from the voice of conscience. I couldn't persuade them that this was a sickness rather than a blessing. The trouble with a sensitive conscience is that it often limits your choices, you aren't free to do what the masses around you seem free to do. The trouble with being without a conscience is that there is a deadness, a rottenness at the centre of the life.

But what I've come across almost on a daily basis is an over-sensitive conscience. Like a buoy floating out on the water, it endlessly gongs out its mournful witness. Or a car horn that's stuck and becomes one endless nerve-wrecking blare. A car horn is supposed to scream a word of warning; that's its necessary function. But when it jams it no longer serves its purpose. When the car horn jams everyone knows it's malfunctioning; but when a conscience gets stuck we're tempted to think it's the voice of God from mount Sinai.

Maybe I've misread the situation altogether but I have

the impression that there is a real need for sensitive people to look beyond their flaws and failings and get on with the quest for noble and gallant living. Am I wrong in thinking we spend too much time anguishing over things we're ashamed of but can't seem to change? Aren't there enough of us who can hardly bear to look in the mirror? People whose lives are a moral shambles or who see themselves as trivial and paltry—as pathetic? People who've just about given up on themselves and who feel they have no right to speak to others about the better life and so are no longer socially useful?

It's important, even crucial, for us to be able to live with ourselves while we pursue a life of honour and nobility. We need to resist the seemingly endless stream of self-help books which tempt us to think we're the centre of the universe. But we also need to resist the temptation to wallow in self-pity and self-despising because we're not the noble and gallant people that in our better moments we want to be. Whether we pursue self-fulfilment or wallow in self-despising, we've still put ourselves at the centre and we don't belong there.

That's where good people come in. People who are good and wise and compassionate. These generous people who know how to challenge us without crushing us; who give us credit even for the feeble (but genuine) attempts to live lovely lives and who, while they will not whitewash our wrongs, will not allow our failings to be the final reality. Noble people, whose ultimate aim is not simply to make our lives easier, but following the model given to them by God, they wish to make us braver and cleaner and stronger.

As they pursue this goal and as, bit by bit, they achieve it, they are giving us back our self-respect; enabling us to live with ourselves and therefore making it possible for us to offer hope to others who are in danger of being lost in a world of mirrors and paralysed by self-hate.

In this little book I'd like to add my praise to all those who've made it a part of living to help people regain their self-respect. They've little to learn from the book since they're already living what the book is commending but at least they'll know that people like myself are grateful for their life-style. I even hope that some of the stories might reach some strugglers and help them to believe that life isn't over till it's over. And then, there's that large contingent of fine people who have grown weary in the service of others. Maybe something here will be used by the Spirit of God to fill the limp sails of their lives and give them renewed energy and direction to sail back out into life and the work of rescue.

Arthur Gordon wrote one of the loveliest little books it's been my privilege to read—*A Touch of Wonder*. In the introduction he said what goes double for this lesser book of mine: 'Please don't look in the pages for firm organisation or neat chronology. A book of this kind can be read backward or forward or even sideways. You can start at the beginning or the end.'

SECTION ONE:
COMPASSION

ONE

The struggler's need of compassion

Matheson had preached for about fifty years when they asked him what he would change if he had to do it all over again. He said he would 'make it more kind.' He saw that the mass of people struggled with troubles enough without him making it harder. My own very limited experience confirms that.

With everyone else I believe in justice but when we're not outraged by degenerates and brutes, when we're calmer and more reflective, we know (or so it seems to me) that life is awfully tough for huge segments of humanity.

The Christian faith not only says we should be compassionate; it says we should be compassionate because that's how God is. The parable of the Good Samaritan not only calls us to be compassionate, it shows us the heart of God. God couldn't just walk on by and leave us in trouble and if we are to live in the image of God we've got to practice God-imitating compassion.

Since he was a keen observer of life, I think Jesus the Messiah, must have taken long looks at donkeys and maybe an occasional camel, burdened to the skies, protesting as they made their way along the roads. Seeing them, He would think of people. And weary oxen, with heavy wooden yokes which rubbed their shoulders raw as they pulled a plough from one end of the field to the other, day after day, must have made Him think of burdened people. Once He said, 'Come unto me all ye that labour and are heavy laden and I will give you rest; take my yoke upon you and learn of Me for I am meek and lowly in heart and you will find rest to your souls; for My yoke is easy and My burden is light.'

Jesus didn't think we should be yokeless since He urged people to submit to His yoke but He didn't come to crush and suffocate. He often viewed people as sheep without a shepherd and we're told He had compassion on them.

I don't want people to let me wander through life bruising others and thinking nothing of it; I don't want my unjust behaviour ignored because the people I'm bruising and using need compassion too. (Somebody said there is no kindness so cruel as that which leaves a person a helpless victim to his/her evil.) But while I want chastisement and discipline I want compassionate treatment because, like most people in the world, I'm wounded too and carry burdens I need help with. Since I want this for me, I should want it for others.

While staying in touch with the real world where there are people who really do choose evil as their good and good as their evil, we still need to see fellow-humans as not only sinners but as sinned against. Without losing touch with the need for clear moral judgement we need to have something of the spirit of one of Victor Hugo's characters of whom he said:

Section One: Compassion

The world to him was like an immense malady. He sensed fever everywhere, sought out affliction and without seeking to answer the riddle did what he could to heal the wound.

TWO

Death at thirty-two

About two hundred years ago (or was it yesterday?) Alice lived two doors away from us. She didn't profess to be a Christian and those of us who knew her well knew she had struggles, like the rest of us, which she didn't always win. But Christ loved her. And, Christian or not, he worked in her life, making her cheerful, sensitive, sympathetic and sharing. Like so many others she had a hard life. She had four children, serious heart trouble and a hard-drinking husband who gave her many a beating.

I can still see her in the street, leaning against her window with her arms folded, wisecracking with the neighbours, milkmen or anyone who showed the slightest interest in being friendly. More than once I caught her crying, wondering how she was going to get through the week with so little money and so many things to be done with it. She was thin, too thin, but her skin was so clear and smooth, almost transparent. And her eyes were beautiful, pale blue and big and round. She died undergoing her second heart surgery. I think she was thirty-two-years-old.

Alice reminded me of all the people I had ever known who, day after day, *without end*, struggle to keep their heads above water. *Never*, in all their lives are they able to go to a shop and buy something without first doing serious arithmetic. *Never*, from the cradle to the grave, are they sure the money for the rent, heat, food and clothing is going to be there! It's that endless grind that beats so many people; that takes the light out of their eyes. They march up from the gates of birth with the sunshine on their faces, dreaming dreams, purposing purposes, but life just wears them down. Then we put them in the ground at the age of thirty-two, sadly look at each other and shrug in helplessness.

It's when thoughts like these come tearing their way into your consciousness that you hungrily search for moments when you did something comforting, something kind, something that brought a smile or a happy, speechless look of gratitude. *Not* so that you can brag and think you weren't such a bad neighbour after all. No, its just that it becomes important to know that she didn't die without a moment when she knew somebody cared; that she didn't die never having had friendly arms to hold her while she sobbed. It's at times like these that the heart remembers and is glad for all the 'trivial' moments when cups of sugar were loaned or borrowed or 'quarters of tea' were halved. And a Christian would tell you that the whole story has not yet been told.

THREE

The habit of finding fault

I recall a number of years ago telling my older son, 'Jim, I know I'm making mistakes along the way. I'm not always right but I always have your welfare under consideration. Well, most of the time. But this is my first shot at this adventure. I've never had a sixteen-year-old son before.' And then there was Linda. I made mistakes with her too. But I had no practice runs. I had never been father to a fifteen-year-old girl. All of this was, 'on the job training'. We parents mean well. We're selfish, impatient, demanding and at times suffocating. But parents who love their children wish them no injury; and want only the best for them. 'Remember me, not for what I've done; but for the other things I always meant to do.' Seeing your mistakes can really take the wind out of your sails. Kids don't need parents who are indifferent. What a lonely world it is for a young person when they feel that mum or dad are not at all interested. Nor do children need authoritarian parents who run the home like some army camp for new recruits. Balance isn't easy to find. That's because we're anxious for the best for our children and if they haven't sense enough to see that we can become irritated and act authoritarian and so the seed is sown for a lot of pain in years to come. Sometimes fathers catch a glimpse of themselves overdoing it and it wrings from them the confession of Livingston Larned (I've adapted it a little).

Listen, son, I'm saying this as you lie asleep, one hand crumpled under your cheek...I've stolen into your room alone. A few minutes ago, as I sat reading my paper, a stifling wave of remorse swept over me, I had been cross with you. I scolded you as you were dressing for school because you only dabbed your face with a towel. I chewed on you for not cleaning your shoes. I spoke angrily when you threw some things on the floor. I found fault at breakfast too. You spilled things, gulped your food, put your elbows on the table, put too much butter on your bread. As I left for work you waved and called, 'Good-bye, Daddy!' and I told you to straighten your shoulders. The same thing in the afternoon. As I came up the road I saw you, down on your knees playing marbles. There were holes in your socks. I humiliated you before your friends by marching you ahead of me to the house. Socks were expensive—if you had to buy them you'd be more careful. Imagine that from a father! Do you remember, later, when I was reading my paper, how you came in, a bit timidly? I impatiently asked you, What do you want? You didn't say a thing. You threw your arms around my neck and kissed me. And you held me with an affection that God has set in your heart and which even neglect hasn't withered. Then you were gone, pattering upstairs to bed. It was shortly after that that I felt the guilt and sickening fear. I've got into the habit of finding fault, regimenting, rebuking. This is my reward to you for being a boy. It wasn't that I didn't love you; it's that I expected too much of a boy. I was measuring you by the yardstick of my own years. And there is so much in you that is good and fine and true. Your enormous heart which showed itself in your coming to kiss me goodnight in spite of everything. Nothing else matters tonight, son. I'm here kneeling by your bedside, ashamed. You wouldn't understand any of this if I told you about it. But tomorrow I'll be a real daddy. I'll be your chum; suffer when you suffer and laugh when you laugh. I'll bite my tongue when impatient words come. I'll keep saying: 'He's nothing but a little boy—a little boy!' I'm afraid I visualised you as a man. But looking at you now, crumpled and weary in your bed, I see you're only a little boy. Yesterday you were in your mother's arms. I've asked too much, too much.

FOUR

Give me the lad
that's gone

Davie was about eight years older than me. To an eleven-
or twelve-year-old kid this well-dressed, charismatic and
handsome guy was someone to be envied. He was a bit of
a wild one but we all grinned at much of his wildness. He
was something of a hero to most of the kids I hung around
with. He had always dabbled with booze but I began to
notice him being drunk more and more often. Then he'd
get in more and more street fights. Not very long after that,
Maggie his fiancé, decided to drop him. He went down like
a stone. I began to see less and less of him. The next time
I saw him, a few years later, he was a chronic alcoholic. He
went from one hospital to the next and then into a hospital
for the mentally unstable. Just yesterday as I was driving
down a busy main street in Belfast, an old man ran right out
in front of me. He was clutching a bottle in a brown paper
bag, his hair was as white as the driven snow. I didn't hit him
but as he lurched away I looked into his face — it was Davie.
Old too soon. And *lost*! Not just lost in some narrow
religious sense. Lost to health, lost to self-respect, lost to
Maggie, lost to his parents, lost to marriage and a family
with children, lost to dreams that should be dreamed, to

noble deeds that should be done, to noble thoughts that should be thought. Gone all of the possibilities of his manhood. Lost to friendship. Lost to himself. And Oh sweet Lord, lost to you too. And somehow I feel responsible. If you asked me how I wouldn't be able to tell you. But the feeling's there. I feel a deep sense of personal loss even though we were never friends. Is that why I feel responsible? *Because* we were never friends? Maybe all this is just foolishness, but somehow, I feel we've all suffered loss in the loss of Davie.

He must live in one of the multitude of hostels scattered throughout Belfast. I wonder if every now and then he might sit alone in the dark missing the Davie he once knew, wondering how he got into this shape and wondering how he'll ever get out of it or even if he'll get out of it at all.

With the departure of Bonnie Prince Charlie thousands in Scotland saw a dream die; saw hopes smothered and glory missed. In the young prince's failure they saw their own and one of their poets sadly wrote:

> *Sing me a song of a lad that is gone,*
> *Say, could that lad be I?...*
> *Give me again all that was there,*
> *Give me the sun that shone!*
> *Give me the eyes, give me the soul,*
> *Give me the lad that's gone...*
> *Billow and breeze, islands and seas,*
> *Mountains of rain and sun,*

All that was good, all that was fair,
All that was me is gone.

I miss Davie, somehow. And I think of all the other Davies who hang around corners. And I can't completely rid myself of guilt feelings that I should be so blessed and others lost. I'm determined by the grace of God to do more than the little I'm doing to 'justify' my having so much. Ah, Davie, Davie.

FIVE

Someone who understands

Wasn't it Emerson who said that we all cry out for someone to understand us? Man's deep need in this area is part of the Christian doctrine of 'the Incarnation'. A Bible passage says that Jesus Christ partook of flesh and blood because that's what humans are. And He did it, the passage says, that He might become an understanding and faithful high priest. I like that message. More to the point, I need it.

No decent person, Christian or non-Christian, wants people to whitewash their wrongs. In our better moments we all want to shoulder the responsibility for our moral failures. They're doing us no favours who persuade us we have no guilt to bear. Unless we face our sin (or if you don't like that word, and can't begin there, substitute another and start from there), there is no deep peace either here or hereafter. So when I speak of 'understanding' I'm not talking about a whitewash job. Still, the pressure to do wickedly is very strong and unceasing and it's a fool who expects the 'Prince of Darkness' to be run off by a simple wish of ours. He's had thousands of years of practice in seducing and weakening people—he didn't become the 'god of this world' for nothing. And it's a joy to hear the message that God in Christ understands the pressure and assures us that He will never fail us nor forsake us as we pursue a noble heart and gallant lives.

The story I heard when I was young was about this ten-year-old kid who had saved up all his money—but it didn't amount to much. He wanted a dog, real bad! He made his way out to the farm where he knew dogs were bred and he approached the owner with his request. 'I want to buy a dog!' he said as he pressed his money into the breeder's hand and turned to look through the wire-mesh fence. Said the man, 'Son, this isn't nearly enough. These dogs cost twenty times this amount.' The boy hardly looked at him and said, 'That's all my money. Please, I want to buy a dog.' The owner protested but the boy looked at him earnestly and said he had no more and could he please have a dog. Further talk didn't move the young man but it moved the older one. He brought the child inside the fence, opened a wooden gate and out cascaded a mass of grateful, frisky, handsome pups. The child gave them a good looking over and then made a bee-line for one with a back leg that was crippled in some way. The man, thinking the boy chose the injured one because he had so little money, assured him he didn't have to take that one; that he could have whichever one he wanted. But the boy wanted *that* one and he explained: 'Well, he has a bad leg, don't you see, and so do I' (pulling up his trouser leg to reveal his skinny leg wrapped in a metal brace), 'so he'll need someone who understands to help him live with it.'

I don't want my wickedness ignored, I want it dealt with. I don't want my weaknesses explained away, I want them met head on. But I'm terribly in need of someone to help me live with what I'm struggling with. Every time we come across someone who believes it is part of living to be sympathetic—genuinely helpful, but compassionate—God is reminding us of how He is. 'That's what I'm like, only more so,' you can hear Him say. I must try to remember the child and the dog. What is it the Lord said? 'Out of the mouths of babes…'?

SIX

Bill the peacemaker

In 1891 a disagreeable student with a bitter tongue earned the name 'Bill the Cynic'. He wrote to a friend he had offended, 'I know I am hard, proud, conceited, scornful, bitter... and insulting very often, and always selfish; but I don't like you to treat me as though I wasn't trying to do a bit better.' Now there's pain! Yes, I know he inflicted pain. I'm not trying to deny what everyone under the sun knows! I only wish to stress a point not often enough stressed. (Well, it seems under stressed to me.)

Rebukers often get to enjoying the process. Transgressors are very often stripped of their flesh, centimetre by centimetre until they are a quivering mass of exposed nerve-endings. The shock to the nervous system is more severe than many can appreciate. It takes such a long time to recover from an experience like this. Some never really do. Their possibility for growth is blasted and their life becomes one nervous recoil after another. The rebukers mercilessly strip them because, 'they must be made to see and feel the seriousness of their transgression.'

It makes no sense at all to strip and traumatise and further shame those who give every indication that they're fully aware of their guilt. And how I detest the accusation, 'She's only sorry because she got caught.' What an unkind thing to say when there's not a shred of evidence to substantiate it. What arrogance we show by this claim to be able to see behind sobs and a burning face. God protect us from these clairvoyants who 'know' the inner motivations of others.

And it isn't unusual for the rebuker when he warms to his work to accuse the transgressor of additional wrongs and of callousness in connection with the wrong. And a sad thing is, the transgressor is often afraid to protest these unjust accusations lest he be thought impenitent, lest doubt be cast on his sorrow in the matter in which he is truly guilty. ('When I talked with him about it he started arguing about side issues. Missed the whole point. Gave me the impression he wasn't really convinced of his wrong-doing or that it mattered much.')

Our opening quotation came from a man called Edward 'Bill' Wilson who accompanied Robert Scott to the Antarctic, and to death. In March, 1912, Scott wrote this of Wilson while they were both waiting death:

> *If this letter reaches you, Bill and I will have gone out together. We are very near it now; and I should like you to know how splendid he was at the end, everlastingly cheerful and ready to sacrifice himself for others...*

The expedition team called him 'Bill the Peacemaker'. It was right in the early days to rebuke him when the occasion warranted it; it was wrong to treat him as though he 'wasn't trying to do a bit better.' The truth is, he'd been trying all along.

And if you believe in a coming Judgement when all wrongs will be righted there is added reason to do in meekness what must be done. For on that day, the one we will meet up with won't be the dry-mouthed, spluttering punch-bag we once confronted. It will be the Champion of the wronged party. Someone who will look strangely like all the guilt-ridden people we expertly butchered back in long-forgotten days.

SEVEN

A card around his neck

C. S. Lewis confessed that he didn't especially enjoy the company of little children. This is a bit surprising but not to the discredit of that wonderful man. Francis Xavier, on the other hand, had a healthy obsession with children. He would work a minimum of sixteen hours a day but more often he would work twenty. Once when he was exhausted he went to his tent to rest for an hour, telling those around him that he didn't wish to be disturbed no matter who asked for him. A few minutes later he rushed out of his tent and said, 'I didn't mean a child. If it's a child, wake me immediately.' Both Lewis and Xavier knew that children were too important to be neglected. Too important even to leave the raising of them exclusively to their parents. Once children begin to spend more time at school and play than they do in the presence of their parents there is a special need for non-family members to look after them. Mould the child and you mould the world; sin against the child and you sin against the world. There's no change without ideas and truths but ideas and truths come wrapped up in people. Relationships with people either redeem us or damn us and the most fundamental relationships are those of home. It's comforting to know that the world outside our homes, while it has its dangers, has its good people who care for children who are not their own.

The author, L. A. Banks, tells a lovely story of something that happened years ago on a journey across America. Here's what happened. A pale, weepy, little boy looks wistfully down the train where a mother and her laughing children are having something to eat. A man across from him notices his distress and asks him if he has anything to eat. He says he's had some food but he isn't hungry. 'I'm just a bit lonely,' he says, 'there's lots of them over there', nodding at the happy clan, 'and... they've got their mother.' he says with quivering lips. 'And you've lost yours, have you?' 'Yes,' he said, and that he was on his way to live with an uncle he'd never seen. A lady from a town some way back had made him some sandwiches and had hung a card around his neck. She told him to show it to the ladies on the train but he hadn't been able to do that. He told the man he could read it if he wanted to and so he pulled it round from inside his coat. It had his name and address on it and below that it said: 'Whosoever gives even a cup of cold water to one of these little ones, verily I say unto you, he shall in no wise lose his reward.' The man made his way to the family and before you know it George finds these gentle arms around him and the woman's voice, with that soothing tone, calling him poor, dear little fellow and begging him to come with her to her children.

I love it when children meet adults who mean them no harm, who pity them in their vulnerability and who go out of their way to make things easier as well as better. I love it when women, like that one, took the trouble. It isn't her child so why should she bother? Mother Teresa is right, the world's greatest tragedy is *unwantedness*, the world's worst disease is *loneliness*. These two people on the train couldn't sit idly by and watch a child bear his pain alone and while there was a limit to what they could do, they did what they could under the circumstances.

I once read a story about a teenage boy who found himself in terrible trouble. His family had thrown him out, he landed in a foreign country where he had made a go of it until somebody lied about him and he ended up in prison. He told the jailer he was innocent and that his family had mistreated him—the whole story. I don't know if the jailer believed his story or not. (I'm sure he'd heard his share of 'hard luck' stories, of prisoners being 'stitched up' etc.) Anyway, he took the young man under his wing, treated him with extraordinary kindness and when the story ended the boy had become prime-minister to the whole nation as well as the one who saved that part of the world from famine. (The teenager's name was Joseph.) Why did the jailer bother? It wasn't his boy and I'm sure he had plenty to worry about with a job as responsible as his. He did it for the same reason the people on the train helped young George. There are some people who just can't stand by and do nothing while children are enduring pain. I hope my grandchildren, Jason, Cari, Erin, Alison, Kathleen and Zachary, when they're in trouble and their loving parents aren't around—that they find the kind of people Joseph and George found.

EIGHT

Show Him your hands

Mary was a young girl when she died. Her parents were both gone when she was still a child herself so it was up to her to be mother to her brothers and sisters. She worked too hard, slept too little, ate poorly and worried endlessly. Over the years it took its toll. Just before she died, she expressed real concern about meeting Christ because she felt she had done nothing big and brave for him in gratitude for his blessing her and the other children throughout her short life. She was agitated and weepy and said she didn't have anything to offer Him. One of her brothers who was sitting on the bed stroking her thin fevered fingers said, 'You could show him your hands.' I don't know what the young man's total theology might have been or grew to be; I do know, young or not, he'd got to one of the centres of God's concern. Mary's hands were old to soon. When they should have been making daisy-chains they were washing clothes, when they should have been pushing a swing in a playground they were scrubbing floors and cooking meals. I can't abide a religion which says none of this matters! Or a religion which is dismissive of this kind of truth by immediately warning us against 'salvation by works' or the need for 'sound doctrine' as well as an upright life. For pity's sake, we all know that 'legalism' is heresy.

I'm like everyone else (without exception!), there are truths I cannot deny and there are truths I will not hear attacked without defending them (where it seems profitable). *Truth* matters! God has not required us to 'park our brains' in order to please him, in fact, He has called us, biblically, to engage our intellects as well as our passions. Tear-jerking stories are no substitute for reasoned discourse; lies which tug on the heart-strings can never replace justified claims of truth. Someone greater than all of us said it is *truth* that frees. So I'm aware of the need for 'propositional truth' but I'm ashamed when we 'lovers of truth' love only the truth *we* tell, love especially the truths *we* hold distinctively and glibly bypass spell-binding self-sacrifice with a 'Yes, but what do they believe?' Truth is for *doing*! Theological truth is to enable us to live sacrificial lives and a little theology goes a long way when it is creatively applied.

There's more to being an imitator of God than holding correct views and this is especially true when the 'views' are hard to relate to genuine social concerns. The cartoon offers this: A man is sitting in a hotel room, his hair is a mess, his shirt is lying open and his tie is loosed, he's unshaven, his eyes have deep, dark rings around them and he has a look of desperation on his face as he hoarsely says into the phone: 'Pastor, you've got to help me. I've lost my job, my wife has left me, the kids gave gone with her, I'm in debt over my head and I won't be able to pay the hotel bill. Please, tell me, is Revelation 20 literal or figurative?'

Philosophy professor, Christina Sommers, in a lecture on ethics, rehearses a story from Saul Bellow's collection of traditional Jewish stories. There is this rabbi, the story is told, in a small Jewish town in Russia who disappears each Friday morning for several hours. His devoted disciples boast that during those hours their rabbi goes up to heaven and talks to God. A stranger moves into town and he's sceptical about all this so he decides to check things out. He hides and watches. The rabbi gets up in the morning, says his prayers and then dresses up in peasant clothes. He grabs an axe and off he goes into the woods, cuts some firewood which he then hauls to a shack on the outskirts of the village where an old woman and her sick son live. He leaves them the wood which is enough for a week and then sneaks back home to his own house. The story concludes that the newcomer stays on in the village and becomes a disciple of the rabbi and whenever he hears one of the villagers say, 'On Friday morning our rabbi ascends all the way to heaven,' the newcomer quietly adds, 'If not higher.'

Christians will tell you there is another Jewish rabbi who really did ascend all the way to heaven and who would be thrilled at the behaviour of the Russian rabbi. Of this rabbi, one of those who knew him best wrote, 'He went about doing good and healing all that were oppressed by the devil, for God was with him'. It is that Jewish rabbi, Jesus Christ, who claims that one day He will judge the world

(Matthew 25) and on that day one of the central concerns will be what we *did* with truth. Our destiny will hang on whether or not we cared for and catered to the needs of others. Maybe the first question won't be, 'what are your views on this or that issue?' but 'may I see your hands?'

NINE

Selling and smelling

I was on my way to play squash with my friend and tough competitor, Len Moffat. He's the kind who won't stop playing until the match is over and we're back in the dressing room so it was going to be another exhausting session. To give me an edge I skipped lunch but on the way up the hill to the club I passed this couple, sitting on a park bench eating fish and chips. Breakfast had been a long time ago and the smell of their food nearly drove me crazy. Without a word I stopped about two feet from them, licking my lips and devouring the aroma. They smiled at each other and said to me: 'Want some?' With tremendous will-power I turned them down but I went off with that lovely smell filling my thoughts. (It ruined my game. He beat me like a drum. I should have eaten. Yes, that's it. I was too weak. I should have eaten.)

That couple didn't have to say a word about their fish and chips—they sold themselves. The aroma did it. The trouble with so many of us religious people is, we spend more time 'selling' than 'smelling'. (Even when we present the Bible to people, we're always stressing it's 'authority'. We take one legitimate aspect of it and shut out all its winsomeness, its adventure and warmth.) There's a place for speech, sure, but even the speech has to have a winsomeness about it if it's to do any good. I've argued enough in my day to know that argument comes a long way behind aromatic living. An ancient writer, Paul of Tarsus, spoke of Christians as 'the aroma of Christ.' That's a graphic phrase, isn't it? Christians are supposed to 'talk' and 'walk', to 'sell' and 'smell'. The speech and the behaviour are to blend together and make the offer of Christ appealing to discerning and needy people.

The soldier lay dying and the preacher came to attend to him. 'Can I help you in any way?' the young preacher asked. 'I'm cold!' snapped the dying man, 'you don't have a blanket, do you?' In silence the minister took off his overcoat and spread it over him. The dying one glared at him a while. 'My neck is hurting,' he snarled in pain, and off came the minister's other coat to become a pillow. A few more moments of glaring and then in a softer tone: 'What about a cigarette?' The preacher lit him a cigarette and put it in his mouth. Moments of silence, a softening of heart despite the cold and the pain and then he said to the conscientious and obviously sad young preacher, 'Mister, if you've got anything in that Bible that makes you act like this, read it to me.' He had a message to share but sometimes words on their own aren't welcome.

It's for believers to create a healthy hunger in those with whom they have influence. Children need to see lives worth imitating, they need to feel warmth which makes them feel assured and they need to see faith which survives the storms of life. Non-believers have a right to see glad-hearted justice modelled before them by believers, they need to see the words and hymns and prayers matched by honest endeavour, they need to hear quick and genuine confession when the believer has been wrong. Only when they see what it is they feel the need of, only when they encounter what stirs the hidden hunger in them will they be really open to our speech. Believers don't have to be Jesus to get our attention, we will forgive them their failings, but they must be honest failings and there must be honest confession and contrition where that is required. The most persuasive salesman in the world couldn't persuade us to buy after-shave or perfume that smells like sewage water. Should that surprise us? We've got to live the balance and blend 'selling' and 'smelling'.

Of course, Christians need to remember that they have a story to tell and that it's the story and the One who is the centre of the story that redeems and not the aromatic living of the disciples. The lovely life of a Christian only makes sense within the context of that story so we're not permitted just to 'smell'. It's imperative that we *tell* as well as 'smell'.

TEN

Duz your majesty know...

Many years ago, on the west coast of Ireland, a pompous marquis went out for a walk so that people could see him. A boy in short trousers, one sock up and another down, his cloth cap at a rakish angle, passed the marquis with hardly a glance. Offended by the boy's lack of appreciation of his importance, the man thundered after him: 'Boy!' Frightened eyes looked at the human volcano as it thundered: 'Do you know who I am?' A trembling response, 'No, sor, indade I do not.' 'Well, I'm the marquis!' With a respectful touch of the cap the enlightened boy said: 'Pleased to meet yur honour, sor.' Satisfied, the official resumed his parade through the village. Fast recovering, our hero let him get some distance away before he shouted after him, 'And duz yer majesty know who *I* am? I'm Willie John Murphy, from the house down by the bog. That's who *I* am!' And off he went with his shoulders straighter and his thumbs hooked in his braces. A healthy sense of one's personal worth is essential to full and joyful living and Willie John wanted the marquis to know that he wasn't the only one due some respect.

And there's something senseless as well as distasteful

42

about snobbery or elitism. It equates wealth with character, pedigree with personal worth, education with wisdom. It foolishly implies that those who are poor are
pathetic, that those who aren't physical marvels are to be
pitied, that those who don't have a full academic education
are ignorant. What nonsense it is to be arrogant because
you happened to be born into a prominent family or to brag
because you inherited the genes which enable you to be a
great physical specimen. How pathetic it is to see someone
strut because his inherited creed has more truth in it than
someone else's. How blind are those who swagger because
they buy their clothes at a certain shop or attend a particular
school. As though they were 'self-made' people; as though
their blessed situation made them 'class' people.

But sad as all that is, it's sadder still, perhaps, that we
allow people to intimidate us with labels on jeans or the
make of their car. Yes, I know what it is to feel embarrassed
by the brains or beauty or wealth or popularity of others.
But *why* is it so? Why *should* it be so? We 'understand' this
too easily. Superficial explanations as to *why* are too quickly
accepted. We should press for answers until the word is
formally uttered, 'There's no good reason!' And there *is* no
good reason! And because this is so we should refuse to bow
to this tyranny; should oppose it wherever we meet it and
'live' it down.

A healthy sense of personal worth is an adequate de-
fence against all forms of elitism. Those whose views are
worth taking seriously are those who recognise that character is what counts, it's what makes a man or woman
'great'. It has nothing to do with their bank balance or

where they take their holidays but it has everything to do with integrity, kindness and generosity of heart.

But that doesn't go deep enough either because there are many weary men and women who long for cleaner, braver or calmer lives; people whose battles with the darker sides of themselves have been too long with too little success. A moral snob can drive these people into a red-faced tremble. Our sense of personal dignity and worth must be grounded on bedrock or it will be eroded. And that, the Christian would say, is where God's love for us and trust in us is so meaningful and strengthening. In creating humans, in becoming a human and in seeking the rescue and enriching of humans God has made it clear that for Him they are *all* precious and of incalculable worth.

ELEVEN

The hero and Mrs. McIntyre

To feel *wanted*. To believe that there's someone who'd be deeply pained if you weren't there. To suppose, most of the time, that you *really* make a difference. To know tender moments when someone holds you, tender lips softly against your cheek, and whispers that life would be so empty without you! To live without this is hardly to live at all. In a world of throw-away things, it's easy for sensitive souls to feel they're like paper plates or plastic forks.

Family members can make one another feel like they're temporarily useful but permanently dispensable. 'I'm an unpaid servant in my home, all I'm good for is washing, cooking and cleaning! A "home help" would suit them just as well,' the woman sobbed. 'They see me as the "bread-winner",' he said with a sigh. We sorely want to be wanted as well as being thought useful (though we need to be thought useful). It's a terrible blow to us to feel 'used' and not 'wanted'. Those who make us feel both are doing us a great service; they're saving our lives.

If you think that to brighten up someone's *life* is too big a job right now, make up your mind to brighten their *day*! Make them feel they have something to offer; that they enrich your life; that, somehow, just knowing they're in this world with you makes the challenges and the pains easier to bear and the joys that much more joyous. That they make a difference!

Jerry Harvill told us that Marjorie Byrd, the novelist, was visiting the MacIntosh's home in the western Highlands of Scotland. A gale was howling around the cottage, which lay outside the village and Mr. MacIntosh was out. At the height of the fierce storm therewas a knock on the door. A family friend, a young lad, severely crippled and drenched to the skin, had walked from the village to check on Mrs. MacIntosh. She brought him in to warm by the fire and Marjorie Byrd commented on the howling wind. 'Aren't you afraid?' the boy asked intensely. The novelist was about to say 'no' when Mrs. MacIntosh spoke the words every boy longs to hear. 'Of course we were afraid,' she said, 'but now you're here it's all right because we have a man in the house.' The boy straightened his twisted frame, looked at the two women, and said with a firm voice: 'Well then, I'd best be checking to make sure everything is snug.'

Christians will tell you that Jesus Christ had this quality. That without being naïve or unrealistic He could look past the failures of the people He knew and gladly, warmly express His gratitude for what they gave to Him (Yes!). See Luke 22:28 and carefully note the context of the remark. (Now, what am I going to do about what I've just written?)

TWELVE

Pretend you know me

J. H. Jowett called Jesus a 'receiver of wrecks'. I love that. But there are millions of people in each generation who live their lives without getting involved in things that blasted their lives apart. Not everyone is a 'prodigal son' who has ended up in a pig-pen and eating pig-food. The return of a prodigal is beautiful and joy-bringing but it makes no sense to say it is more satisfying and lovely than a boy or girl who never wallowed in shame and degeneracy. Jesus' parable in Luke 15 shouldn't be understood to say otherwise. It's finer and nobler that people resist the call of the 'far country' and live in loving submission to God. It's true that we're *all* sinners and *all* (without exception) are in need of forgiving grace, but it isn't true that we've all wallowed in moral filth to the extent that life became a sewer. And while it's true that God can make great use of those who've plumbed the depths of depravity He rejoices in that redeeming grace restores them to forgiveness and honourable living and we mustn't give the impression that to miss 'the pig-pen' is a disadvantage. Those of us who've wallowed in muck and led others to join us, know what it means to look at the lives of gallant and honourable people and wish we had not been so crassly wicked.

But having said all that, the joyous amazement of moral wrecks who have been welcomed home is something to behold. More amazing, is to hear that it is someone as holy, as clean and as noble as the God of our Lord Jesus Christ who welcomes them home—with joy! This is precisely what offended one of Christianity's early critics, Celsus. He looked at these disciples of Christ and observed that they were all nobodies, ex-criminals and slaves. There was hardly an honourable person among them. And as far as society viewed things, at least in Corinth, that the famous apostle Paul saw it as Celsus saw it. He reminded the Corinthians that there were very few 'big names' among them. Wasn't it John Bunyan who said he was glad that John 3:16 said 'whosoever'? If it had said 'John', he remarked, 'I would have thought it was some other John; but since it said "whosoever" that let me in.'

The story goes that though he was an alcoholic and lived with his other fellow-victims of the booze industry on Skid Row, he always insisted he had been a prominent business man before he hit bottom. He 'smelled bad, looked bad, shook bad and dressed bad,' but he always told stories of better days; days of respect, wealth and influential friends. His fellow-victims didn't believe a word he said. 'You were always nothing, you're nothing now and you'll always be nothing!' they told him and this just unzipped him. The more they scorned him the more he felt the need to tell his story. (I don't know if he was telling the truth.)

One day while he told his story and they mocked him he

saw an obviously successful man walk down the street on the other side. Desperation made him claim he knew the man, that they had been close in former years. That was a mistake because they called him a liar and urged him to prove it by approaching the stranger. What to do? He felt he had no option. He hurried across the road and with great urgency he quietly said: 'Please, mister, I'm sorry to bother you...I don't want any money...but please, will you pretend you know me? *Please!*' A quick glance at the gawking living-dead told the man what had happened and he sensed the desperation in the one before him. He let out a whoop, threw his arms around him, slapped his back, nearly shook his hand off his shoulder and said (loud enough): 'I haven't seen you in years. I wondered where you'd gotten to. How on earth are you managing?' He took him down the road, cleaned him up, got his hair cut, suited him out and fed him till he thought he'd burst and put some money in his pocket. The rich man went on his way and the drunk back to Skid Row but now he had substance for his stories. Someone had refused to be ashamed of him. I don't know who the rich man was but he helped me just by showing such compassion.

I know life is complex and things aren't easily changed. I know simple acts of individual compassion and kindness don't change the whole of society. I know that simplistic approaches to pain and poverty can turn out to be 'benevolent bungling'; but I also know that it's too easy to convince ourselves that we shouldn't reach out and do crazy, compassionate acts. Many of us are 'too wise'; we see the complex issues too clearly and are able to critically appraise the pros and cons of acting on our feelings. Our appraisals are accurate, clinical, wise and barren. We're never conned, never embarrassed by our enthusiasm, we never feel sheepish or foolish for having acted so passionately or spontaneously. We're everywhere known as the 'wise' ones who take our responsibilities 'seriously'. We're never in the situation where we are speechless when asked to explain 'inexplicable' behaviour. In short we are proper, deliberate, methodical and dispassionate—and barren.

There was One who came, refusing to be ashamed of us. Who offers us not only a meal, clothes, a bath and a temporary release. He offers us his name, His permanent cleansing, and a permanent home—we need not go back to what we were. And He makes this offer and bears the burden of this offer in the person of those who are is disciples. They are the instruments of His compassion and rescue. How could it be otherwise?

SECTION TWO:
ENCOURAGEMENT

ONE

The struggler's need of encouragement

We need more than pity if we are to grow strong and have a healthy self-respect. We need people to challenge us as well. People to make demands on us and who will not allow us to develop into snivelling wimps. People who refuse to let us give up the battle too easily; who call us to greater efforts to gain what we know is honourable. People who inspire us to be brave! People whose very example makes demands of us.

It isn't always helpful to tell people they're OK the way they are! Sometimes they need the courage to face themselves, recognise their need for change and get on with it. It isn't loveless to confront, if that's what we judge is needed. C. S. Lewis was right when he said that we may love people who are dirty, rude, ungrateful or cruel but we don't love them *because* of these things; we love them (or they us) *despite* these things. And it isn't patronising to help them to change! One who says she loves me and who has no interest whatsoever in helping me to be a richer, finer, nobler person needs to think again about what 'love' means. People who love us will work with us to help clean us up.

The atheist, Friedrich Nietzsche, although he admired Jesus (he said Jesus was the only Christian and people murdered him), despised what he saw as Christianity. Christians, he claimed, were weaklings and refuse to make the effort at being strong so they made a virtue out of weakness and a vice out of strength. He would tell people over and over: 'Neglect not the hero in thy soul.' When you look around and within, you're inclined to think the man had a point and we need to accept his challenge.

In the days of the big sailing ships when the sailors came back from a two-year voyage around the world, they'd tell their stories and soon young people would gather round to listen. They wouldn't speak of balmy nights in sheltered harbours, soft breezes, sandy beaches or fun-filled days in calm lagoons. No, they'd speak of awful storms, thirty foot waves that threatened to sink the ship, heroic deeds in the face of terrible danger, tough captains and endless risks. They'd pull off their shirts to show magnificent scars and explain their limp as proof of close brushes with death and country boys, I said, country boys, would forsake their ploughs and run off to sea with a gleam in their eyes.

This is what is missing in to much religion and church-going. We sing soul-stirring hymns, pray earth-shaking prayers, call for world-renouncing commitment and then run around over-fed, over-played and as predictable as next week's bus-schedule. Maybe the world isn't tired of our story. Maybe it's just tired of our pretending we're excited about it when the truth is we are bored out of our minds and act like it!

We need people to sympathise with us and then to call

us back into the business of brave living. We need them to recognise the burdens we bear and the opposition we face but we need them to move us on from there. We don't need them to bully us but they mustn't always be soft, they mustn't be too gentle. They may not be able to change our circumstances but we need them to help us to take courage and to live gallantly within our circumstances, as multiplied millions of people are doing every day in all parts of the world!

We are in desperate need of people who will speak and live before us and make demands on us and restore in us the sense of adventure in living as disciples of Christ. Those who make a confession of Jesus the Messiah are the offspring of men and women who ate the fire that was to burn them, drank the water that was to drown them and fought an indignant world to a standstill

It isn't hard for me to imagine Christ saying to many of you, 'Yes, I know you've been under tremendous pressure for a long time now. I know you've been carrying great burdens and carrying them "alone". And while the rest have had things easy, you've been hurting terribly. I really wish I could take your place for a while just to give you a break but that isn't possible. If our roles were reversed you would feel for Me, deeply, and then you'd urge Me to be brave. That's what I'm urging you to do.'

TWO

One more time

Bernard told me of a childhood incident. The boys would gather around each lunch-time to 'chin the bar', with their girl-friends proudly looking on. The champ could pull his chin over the overhead bar ten times. Little Kenny was doing well if he managed seven. One day, said Bernard, Kenny did seven and tried for eight! Painfully, he managed it, and still held on. The little crowd was astonished as Kenny dragged his tortured body up for another. Now he just hung there, unable to go up but unwilling to let go. The group stood hushed, the champ was nervous and Kenny looked beaten. Then a familiar voice rang out from the back, 'OK now, Kenny, one more time!' (It was his little sister.) That did it! Up he went, almost rupturing his muscles, but he matched the record. That's a great story.

When we're sorely tempted to stop trying in marriage, we need someone to strengthen us with 'one more time'. When in business it begins to look like 'good guys come last' we need an inner voice to challenge us with 'one more time'. When the pain and loneliness has been going on so long that we feel we just can't go on living another day, how we need someone to slip an arm around us and say, 'come on, now, one more time'. When the evil habit seems all-powerful and we're tired of the unending struggle, when we're on the verge of letting ourselves drift with the current we must have someone to keep us going with, 'OK, just one more try.'

She lived up the street from us. She was young, had three children (or was it four?) but she had no husband. We had her in a time or two and she and my daughter Linda seemed to get on quite well. Frequently we'd stop and talk with her briefly on the street. Always quiet and pleasant. She said, 'yes, she would like to visit with us again very soon.' We didn't see her for quite a while and then my wife Ethel asked a neighbour about her. 'Oh, didn't you know?' the neighbour said, 'She took her life.' She'd been hanging on by her fingertips. She couldn't try anymore so she took pills which eased her way out of her painful, lonely world. How we wish we could now say in a practical way, 'come on, now, one more day,' but it's too late.

I'm not saying we should be all-knowing. That isn't possible. I'm only talking about a deeper sensitivity and eagerness to help where we can. We can't always change a person's circumstances but it's possible by 'being there', with looks, words, little kindnesses to help change the person so they can cope with their circumstances. And I know we've failed in this so often and allowed opportunities to slip away but we mustn't retire from the game. Just listen for a moment and you'll hear a voice, like the voice of Kenny's little sister, 'All right now, one more time.'

THREE

'A little something extra'

Sammy Law and his wife Jean lived 'out in the sticks' not far from Coleraine. He had seen combat at close quarters in Korea and were it not for some comrades he would have got more than a bullet in the foot which left him with a limp. His wife Jean was a hospitable soul with the hard tone of many northern country women (but which didn't match her kindness as a host). Like so many other country women she could bake the most delicious bread. Smother it with butter as it came straight from the griddle—a king couldn't eat better. It was Sammy who took me fishing for the very first time in my life.

I spent the night with the Laws, talking into the later hours (as usual). I had barely shut my eyes when Sammy shook me awake to go fishing. It was 4.30 in the morning. I didn't know such an unearthly hour existed until that moment. It was cold, wet, windy and dark as we made our way to the river and I wondered, as I shivered repeatedly, if I was quite right in the head but it was too late to debate the wisdom of the venture. Sammy put a worm on my hook, threw the line out into the dark river and moved off into the shadows down-river. In the early morning quietness I could hear him humming now and then and I could hear the swish of his line as he repeatedly cast it into the river. I was miserable and the worm on my line wasn't even trying. I don't know how long I stood there wishing I was back in bed or at least somewhere comfortable, and then I felt it. A fish was nibbling at the worm on the end of the line and I felt that coming through the line into my hands and from there down to somewhere behind my belly-button. Down there in the dark, beyond my vision, was life, tugging on my line. He ate up all my worm and then took off. The safest meal he ever had, no doubt. But he had made contact with me and that magic moment has stuck with me now for more than thirty years. I reeled in my line, checked to make sure the worm was gone, groped my way down to Sammy and had him put another worm on the line and went back in search of more adventure. I don't remember anything else about that trip but with startling clearness I can recall how I felt before the fish mugged me for my worm and how I felt after he made his hit. Out of the darkness, when I least expected it, when I might have been tempted to think there was nothing there, a gentle tugging told me I was in touch with life and misery became excitement. For those who've fished all their lives and have caught about eleven and a half million fish this may be 'old hat' but it was a magical experience for me.

Now I know this doesn't rank as an 'argument' and I know too that it will make no sense to those who cannot share the faith of a Christian, but I think God watches us and knows that sometimes in life our poor little minds wander, our faith falters, the pressures of life weigh heavily on us to the point where we need 'something more'. My sister Margaret put it this way and I know she was right when she said, 'Sometimes we're in special need of Him. He knows this and He gives us "a little something extra".' God gives us 'a little something extra' to let us know he's there. When we're miserable and really wondering what it's all about, He gives a little 'tug on our line' to let us know we are dealing with *life* when we deal with Him; that we aren't just shivering alone in the dark. A remarkable answer to prayer, an experience so uplifting you can't do anything else but look up and say thank you, an incredible 'coincidence'. And I want you to know, I'm not talking about God getting people parking-spaces that saves them a 90 second walk or God leading people to the right hairdresser. I'm talking about times of inner stress, of loneliness, of weariness when life is pressing down on you, when your heart's breaking, when people are being mean and your soul needs 'a little something extra'. Then there's an arm around the shoulder, someone strokes your hair, a letter out of the blue, a loved one who recovers from illness, a phone call and a whispered and genuine apology that makes the sun shine again, a fear finally dissolved—all 'tugs on the line'. God letting you know he's around. That 'little something extra' which enables you to press on joyfully. Or if not filled with joy, at least, helped by the knowledge that you are seen and cared for. (And for you who are burdened with pain you haven't sought and who haven't yet experienced that 'little something extra'—continue to be brave and be strong to live without it, trust Him still and maybe when the ultimate day arrives, you who were gallant enough to live without 'the tug' will receive 'a little something extra' for being so brave.)

FOUR

The seagull and the storm

As you leave Belfast, going east toward Cultra, Helen's Bay
and Bangor, you quickly come to Holywood. That's where
Ethel and I live, on the coast, and only about four hundred
yards from the Belfast Lough which is part of the Irish sea.
One of the real pleasures of life, for me, is to dress for the
weather and walk along the sea-front on a path I think runs
all the way down the coast as far as any sane man or woman
would want to walk. I like it on our occasional bright days
but I really like it on wild, wet days. I'm a bit afraid of the
sea but I'm fascinated by it just the same, especially when
it's wild—providing I'm not on it. Several years ago a
hurricane which had been off the east coast of America was
moving our way and we were to get the tail end of it. That's
what the meteorological people told us, and that's precisely what we got (and we didn't want any more than
that). I dressed up, made my way to the path down by the
sea and battled the elements. Every now and then I had to
lean into the wind and really work to make some headway;
it was a cracker of a day. The sea was boiling, the rain was
bucketing down and the wind was shrieking like a banshee.

I stopped every now and then hypnotised by the chaos
of the water and that's when I saw him. He was sitting on
a channel marker out in the water and I had to peer intently
to keep a clear picture of him. A seagull. He was sitting out

there, perched on top of a post, supported by skinny little legs. His head and neck were sunk down into his shoulders and he was looking around him with that superior look that all seagulls seem to me to have. As though they scorned everything and everyone in sight. He amazed me with his total indifference to the raging elements around him that tugged at his feathers, shrieked in his ears and threatened to pulverise him. As I watched, an outrageous gust of wind, screaming like a madman hit him full force and lifted him right off the post. But at the very moment the wind knocked him off he spread his wings, used the wind and floated right back to where he was before. Down went the head and neck into the shoulders and back came the scornful look as he glared all around him. I felt like applauding him. I'd just seen a skinny-legged little handful of life spit in the eye of a gale. I'd just watched a vulnerable little bird get what he wanted by using the elements which threatened to injure him. I've seen people do that too.

When I first met Dirk Clay he was a wide-eyed young man who wanted more than anything else to be a preacher. But Dirk had a problem—he had a pronounced stammer and the more nervous he became the more marked the stutter. He actively pursued therapy as well as his ministerial studies but there was no sign of any improvement. Terribly upset, weeping and shaking he came to my study one day and began to pour out his heart, his frustration, disappointment and pain. If God needed ministers to teach people about Him and since Dirk wanted to share those wonderful things, why was it God wasn't curing his speech impediment? I didn't know then and I don't know to this day. I only know we talked and listened to each other. We prayed and young Clay said if God wouldn't correct things, why, then, he would just have to live with it and serve the Lord as best he could. I didn't see him for several weeks after that. The next time I remember seeing him he was sitting on one of the front seats while a Mr. Hollis Maynard was teaching a class of people to speak in sign so that they could learn from and teach the unhearing! That's what he did with his speech impediment! He used it to move him into a ministry where the hearing people, like myself, are dumb. I'll never forget Dirk Clay. It's been years since I've seen him but the last time I saw him he was teaching Bible, fluently, without stammering, on his hands, to people I can't teach and from whom I am unable to learn the many things they have to teach me. He opened up a new world to himself and to the unhearing and so both were blessed. I remembered the remark of the atheist, Nietzsche who said, 'Neglect not the hero in thy soul.' And he insisted, 'What does not destroy me, strengthens me.' But it was from Jesus Christ that Clay learned his life's lesson; from Jesus Christ who assured all the noble-hearted that in a world filled with raging storms they can have peace in him. Such people have found that the very thought of Him has enabled them to bear and use affliction in the service of others. That's how he used His own storm at Golgotha, to bring help and rescue to countless people battered by the storms of life. I enjoyed those walks around the coast but that was one special day; the day I saw a seagull whip a storm!

Applauding the strugglers

I think it was the first time I felt like this. I met Billy Moore whilst in Belgium. I wasn't around him long—alone or with others—before I sensed the man's guilelessness. He was completely open, he spoke with a crisp plainness and he struck me as one who had no hidden agendas. Maybe I'd felt that way before about someone but I just can't remember. I've known and loved him now for some years and I'm still struck by that guileless quality in him. Later we were together in Germany where he preached Christ and I met his wife, Jeanne, and the children. That must have been at least half of forever ago (but maybe it was only yesterday—it's all so vivid). The very thought of these two makes a pleasant life even more pleasant and a life of stiff challenges easier to respond to.

Well, a number of years ago I was with them in Fort Walton Beach where they lived and it was as we were driving home I saw her. I suppose she was in her early seventies, tall, white haired, tanned and healthy looking; but since she was using a walking frame I supposed she was feeble or had been ill. She was behind the gate, in the driveway and as we slowly passed her she smiled this big bright smile and began to applaud as she followed us with her head and eyes. I smiled, waved back and then I asked Billy what the story was.

She was living with her son and daughter-in-law (maybe it was her daughter and son-in-law) and it wasn't unusual for her to be there at the gate, smiling and applauding people passing by. It seemed a little eccentric and I asked him why she did it and he said something to the effect that she thought people have plenty to deal with so she was giving them some encouragement. I wanted to know what her children thought about it. He said they didn't mind it at all. Isn't that a marvellous thing? Here's a lady who has already lived most of her life, must have seen a lot and had known her own share of pain, *applauding the strugglers*. I love it when that memory comes unbidden into my mind every now and then.

Look, I know that to pretend there's no ugliness and evil in the world is sheer nonsense and I know the right response to this corruption is not a weak-kneed indulgence or blind sentimentality. But the older I get the more smitten I am by this truth: people are not only sinners, they're sinned against! They aren't only exploiters, they're victims. At the one end of the spectrum we have the unspeakable evil, on the other end we have the incredibly lovely and in between, in various positions, are the rest of us who stumble along and do the best we can. George Matheson, had preached for fifty years, and when they asked him what he would change if he were to do it all again, he said, 'I'd make it kinder!' If we were wiser, better people we'd try to make it easier for almost all the people we meet. We can't know the burdens people are carrying as they pass us by on the streets but it's a near certainty, that in one area or another, most people are sorely struggling.

I had to go to the post-office so I parked our little vehicle in a side street with Ethel in the back in her wheelchair (she's paraplegic). I came back about five minutes later and she told me of an incident which happened just outside the van window. Here's what happened. There was a betting shop fifty feet away from where I'd parked. A husband with his shabbily dressed young wife and two little children stopped there. She was very thin, palefaced and obviously very nervous. She said to him, 'Why don't you let me go in and put the bet on for you?' He said, 'no'. She said, 'It won't take me long, let me do it.' He snarled at her, 'You don't trust me, do you?' and she timidly said she didn't. He cursed her and belted her hard with the back of his hand on the face before he went in to put the money on a horse. She walked off holding her face and weeping with her wide-eyed children holding on to her long coat. Had I seen her I would have thought of her as one more of the countless young, poorly fed wives and mothers with well-worn clothes, worry-worn features and not a lot of money to go around. Not knowing that she lived with a man who would publicly beat and humiliate her in the presence of the children just because she didn't want him to risk all their money in a bookies, I wouldn't have thought her situation was as hard as in fact it was. I would have pitied her less and expected more from her just because I hadn't all the facts. We *can't* know how deep their pain or how hard their struggle but an educated guess from a compassionate heart would assume that people are terribly in need of encouragement because they bear great burdens. And there are countless ways to give it—we can find them if we want them. One sweet lady did it from behind a walking frame in Fort Walton Beach, Florida and I can't forget that. (And what am I going to do about what I'm writing here?)

SIX

'Your friend, Herbie'

Don Williams told us of something that happened in a little school in Midland, Texas. As I recall it, here's what he said. The seven-year-old boy began his morning by falling off the school bus, cutting his head and needing a couple of stitches. In the break between classes he collided with another little boy. The result? A couple of loose teeth and a split lip. During the afternoon he fell and injured his arm so Mr. Chapman, the school principal, thought they'd better get him home before anything else happened to him. Driving him home the principal noticed he was clutching something in his hand and he asked him, 'What do you have there?' The little boy, all smiles, showed him a shiny quarter of a dollar. 'Where did you get it?' the principal asked him. 'I found it on the play-ground,' they boy said. Then he beams with excitement and pleasure and says to the principle, 'You know, Mr. Chapman, I've never found a quarter before, this is my lucky day!' Don't you love that? A cut head, loose teeth, an injured arm and a split lip—'my lucky day'.

That's the kind of stuff heroes are made of. People who find reason to rejoice in the middle of their pain. People who refuse to be or remain victims. They are not fools, they don't deny the pain in life; they just won't let it be their lord and master. They refuse to endlessly gaze at their troubles until excessive self-pity takes over and ruins them completely. I don't want to make anybody feel guilty about feeling hurt and taking it seriously, I just wish I could say something that would enable those people to get up and go on, see with their eyes the good things of life as well as the evil, the pleasant and joy-bringing aspects of life as well as the crushing experiences. (There is some suffering, so deep, so stark, that words like mine are virtual obscenities. I'm not addressing suffering of that magnitude.)

Do you remember poor Miss Faversham in *Great Expectations*? Jilted on her wedding day, she lived the rest of her life wearing her wedding dress in the very room where she received the awful news. The clocks were stopped at that very hour and all remained precisely as it was. She died years before her death, by fire when it finally came.

And the heroine's father in *A Tale of Two Cities*? After spending years in the dreaded Bastille he was brought to England and freedom. But late at night they would often hear him do what he had been forced to do in the darkness of his cell, mending shoes and mumbling his prison number. He had never been freed—they only moved his body from France to England. Pain can crush and brutalise. It isn't always strengthening or character-building but the kind of pain that most of us have to face, real and sharp and sometimes prolonged, we can overcome. In real life, people like Viktor Frankl, who suffered terribly during 'medical experiments' under the Nazis in their evil camps, have taught us that it isn't what happens to us that ultimately matters but what we do with what happens to us. Glib? Coming from Frankl? No, it's amazing how often one comes across suffering of a horrendous kind only to discover that the sufferer is ablaze with cheerful stubbornness!

In the movie, *Jeremiah Johnston*, the hero wants to be a mountain-man and has to pay an awful price to achieve his goal. He freezes, starves, suffers in loneliness, loses his wife and his adopted son, has to endure a prolonged period of hostility when Indians seek his life as, one after another they come to kill him. Having begun utterly ignorant, completely helpless and an object of derision as a man from 'down below' he becomes known and revered by his former Indian enemies as well as hardened mountain-men. In the closing scene an older man seeks him out living just above the snow-line and as they share a sparse meal the older man says, 'You've come a long way, pilgrim, was it worth all the trouble?' Johnston looks at him and then at the meat and with a dismissive little sound says, 'What trouble?' I love it when I see this kind of thing in great literature and I love it even more when I see it in gallant people about whom they write great literature.

We need brave spirits to change the world. All right, to change communities or individuals, if not the world. People who are realists, who acknowledge pain, their own included. But people who refuse to be intimidated into paralysis. Newton Baker was the U.S. Secretary of War during the first World War and he told of a veteran he came across during one of his regular visits to the casualty wards. The man had lost both legs, both eyes, one arm and his face was horribly burned. He was pushed around the grounds in a wheelchair by a nurse and Baker told of his extraordinary cheerfulness and how that some time later, not only did he live, he married his nurse. (What a woman!) That was the end of the story until some years later when Baker was asked to give a special presentation at the famous John Hopkins University in Baltimore, Maryland, to one of the university's all-time brilliant students. The Ph. D. was to be presented to that crippled and handicapped veteran! Unusual? Yes, of course! But not as rare as you might think.

You've seen the news coverage yourself. A refugee camp, sickness rampant, hunger everywhere, death in every other hut and then some smiling, socially useful (yes!) man or woman who looks all those challenges right in the eye and *lives* in spite of them. Rubbing shoulders with the weeping, despairing and beaten people (*and I have NO criticisms to make of those people*) are the unbowed ones, who come walking out of huge sewer pipes they are using as houses, rags covering each end to keep out the wind—out of these come the suffering, intelligent and realistic souls who won't grovel. All around the world you come across people who choose to live in these conditions so that they can help to ease the burdens of the other sufferers. In a book called *Children's Prayers* one of the children surveyed the challenges and risks that a life of faith in God can bring and wrote God a note, 'Dear God, count me in. Your friend, Herbie.'

SEVEN

The Belfast Ropeworks

I was twenty-one years of age (going on nine) when I worked in the 'Ropeworks'. At our end of the huge shed we produced large rolls of string and the six women who tended the front end of the six big machines were 'piece workers'—the more string they made, the more money they earned. I worked at the back of the machines and my job was to see that they were supplied with the raw materials which came to me in large bins. Sometimes the people supplying me were slow in getting the materials to me and that meant the women had to wait until the supply came and that meant less money. The rule was, whoever ran out of materials first was the first to get a fresh supply. Five of the women lived by that rule and one of them completely ignored it. She would walk round the back, check everyone else's supply and compare it with her own. If she saw it was to her advantage to stop first and get a fresh supply (thus avoiding having to join a line of waiters with perhaps four in front of her), she'd simply scrap the little she had left and say she had run out of material. This was a sly way to jump to the front of the line—she was cheating. What was particularly bad about it, was she knew I knew she did it just about every day and she'd look straight at me as though challenging me to say a noble deed which, for me, in my little fear-filled life, was 'brave'. And, do something about it. What was worse, the five other women knew I knew and knew that I was doing nothing about it. They didn't say anything but they often came round the back when she was cheating and, with a glance, let me know what they knew. I felt terrible about it. Why didn't I stop her? *I was afraid of her*! She had a bad mouth and a look that could have opened a tin of salmon. I couldn't get up the nerve to face her and not only was I guilt-ridden, I was miserable because my gutlessness was known to all those women.

I don't know what it was that morning when freedom came. I vaguely recall having a marked difference of opinion with Ethel and maybe I came into work already heated up with adrenalin flowing. We weren't long into the morning when she came round the back for 'business as usual' but I shouted down the room to her, something like, 'You can leave it as it is; you'll wait your turn like everyone else!' Well, she began to curse me and rant and rave but she was too late—her doormat had tasted freedom! I've never been what you'd call a brave person though I've done a few little things in my life which I'd rank as 'brave' but this was triumph. I felt more like 'Rocky'. I was ecstatic. I felt like running, jumping, shouting. I wanted to go round to the front of the machines and tell all those women what I had done. The depth of my elation embarrassed me since it was such a tiny incident, the kind of thing tens of thousands of people are doing at least once a day without even giving it a second thought. They would shake their heads in bewilderment while I was doing inner handsprings. But it was 'freedom', don't you see. I had shaken off the chains of fear she had bound me with; which I had allowed her to bind me with and now it was as though I could breathe deeply. I felt bigger, taller, more handsome, smarter, as though I owed nobody anything, as though life had begun again with a fresh new start.

I know I was a better person for the next several days; living on the grand feeling, the inspiration of one noble deed which, for me, in my little fear-filled life, was 'brave'. And, maybe, I'm still a stronger, finer person, in some small way because I did what was right on that occasion. I like to think I am, though I'm not yet free of cowardice. Whether any of that is true, this is true—I did what was right and what was needed and what was long overdue and even now when I rehearse it in my mind I feel my heart stir in a deep longing to be like that always.

Now, who is it that you need to kindly but plainly confront that you might enjoy some freedom and peace? Who are they who are depending on you to obtain justice for them? Who is it you need to confront to bring justice to those who depend on you? And how are you preparing to go about it?

EIGHT

I will do more than live

It would appear that some people just insist on being on the whining side rather than the winning side. Everytime they open their mouths it's a bleating session. You'd think the Bible had said, 'Blessed are the *moaners*'. I know for personal reasons that life can be tough and the mass of people really don't complain about people complaining; it's the *whining* that sets them on edge. I must be careful here so as not to confuse genuine and prolonged suffering with once in a while pain but I still must trust the reader to know when they have met up with one or the other. In every city of the world and in every age you read about people who have looked suffering right in the eye and refused to buckle under.

Yvonne and Yvette are thirty-two years old and are joined at the head. They have two independent brains but they share one blood stream. They get on with living.

A 30 degree turn of his head! That's all the control Mark Hicks had of his body but he became a brilliant painter and the movie about his life, *Gravity is my Enemy*, won an Oscar in 1981.

Terry Fox, a twenty-two-year old Canadian, contracted bone cancer which took his leg and finally his life. He ran the 1,800 miles between St. John's and Thunder Bay, with one artificial leg, to raise money for cancer research.

Then there was Helen Keller and Annie Sullivan.

Then there was David Livingstone who began work at ten years of age; working from six in the morning to eight at night. By the time he was eighteen, he had so mastered Latin that he could read Horace and Virgil with ease.

The atheist, Sigmund Freud, lived in constant pain the last sixteen years of his life and endured thirty-three operations. But he stuck to his work to the very end.

Lloyd Ogilvie's friend had lost all vitality and enthusiasm and had become boringly negative. Ogilvie confronted him about it and assured him it was now a choice between degenerating into the grave or living. Weeks later he received a letter of six words: Dear Lloyd, I've decided to live.

This is a tricky area and before we crush everyone with a verbal backhander we need to know the facts. If it's a friend we will search the matter out. If plain talk is what is needed we will speak it. Sometimes we just have to make up our minds to *live* life. William Ward sounded a call that stirs the blood:

I will do more than belong—I will participate
I will do more than care—I will help
I will do more than believe— I will practice

76

I will do more than be fair—I will be kind
I will do more than forgive—I will forget
I will do more than dream—I will work
I will do more than teach—I will inspire
I will do more than earn—I will enrich
I will do more than give—I will serve
I will do more than live—I will grow
I will do more than be friendly—I will be a friend

NINE

No record of wrongs

Four adults sat enthralled by an eleven-month-old boy called Jason. They all hoped he was about to take his first steps. The mother held him upright and the father sat across from him, calling him to come to him. The baby's grandmother watched with bated breath. His grandfather couldn't take his eyes off him (at least in the early stages). Everyone in the room wanted that baby to succeed. Finally after numerous falls without progress, Jason took several steps unaided by anyone. The adults looked at each other in elation. They wanted to see more.

Without their knowing it, I took my eyes off Jason and watched them for a while. My daughter, Linda, was delighted with her baby. My son-in-law, Stan, was bragging away. And my wife, Ethel, the baby's doting grandmother, couldn't get over it. What a boy! I was thrilled with the baby. I was grateful to God that Jason was so blessed. He had people who were really committed to him. They rejoiced in his success. They always will! They knew how many steps he had taken on his own.

I wondered for a few minutes if they could tell me how many times he had fallen and needed lifting. I didn't ask. It seemed such a dumb thought. Just the same, I'm sure they couldn't have told me. They weren't counting how many times he fell; they were interested in how often he was triumphant! I learned something that evening. I saw modelled before me the truth of Hebrews 12:1. The Hebrew writer sees the ancient worthies, as it were, urging us on. Calling us to run the race well. And I saw the truth of 1 Corinthians 13:5 placarded before me. The NIV renders the phrase we're interested in: '(Love) keeps no record of wrongs'. When Peter asked Jesus if forgiving his brother seven times would be enough Jesus told him no. Seventy times seven, was the response of Jesus. He wasn't urging Peter to keep records, He was urging him to forget numbers.

The lady on the phone was really chewing on me. She said, 'That's the second time you've done that!' The sad truth is, she was right. But it did enter my mind as she proceeded to take my flesh off strip-by-strip, that two wasn't the magic number. I didn't say anything, of course, because that would have made it appear that I wasn't particularly concerned that I had done wrong. And I *was* grieved that I had done it. The facts were correct, the spirit was wrong. The poor lady had been keeping a record of my wrongs. Love doesn't do that! This is a hard saying.

And I recognise it as a hard saying (especially if I'm on the receiving end of transgression) but it is the blunt saying of our Lord. Those who care for our souls will rebuke us when we need it but they will not keep an account of evil. I watched the treatment Jason was receiving with pride and pleasure. I contrasted it with what is too often practised—

79

the ignoring of the successes and the recording of the failings. I'm happy for Jason. And I'm happy that throughout the world there are those who will with friendship's hand brush away the chaff in our lives and bring out for inspection, the accomplishments and victories that Christ has blessed us with. And they rejoice in our successes. They acknowledge our mistakes. They're saddened and often hurt by our foolishness. But they 'keep no record of wrongs.'

TEN

A nut on the good side

Do you remember 'Captain Freedom' from the *Hill Street Blues* television series? He was the amateur crime-fighter who wore the circus-tights, the cape, WWI flying helmet, goggles and trainers. He felt 'called' to fight against evil. He carried no weapons. All he had was his physical presence, his words and his innocence. During a shoot-out with the police, armed robbers shot him dead when he jumped up on a car and with his arms raised, shouted: 'Stop this criminal act!' It was only a dumb movie but it had a magic for me; I couldn't get him out of my mind for days. The purity of his intentions, his fearless innocence, the way he risked himself and his vulnerability drew me to the character. Society would call him a 'nut' and in a world of practical and cynical people, 'nuts' have nothing to offer.

And, yet, 'Captain Freedom' was a 'nut' on the good side. It's crazy little people who lay their lives on the line that get close to our hearts or grab sufficient headlines to inspire an unknown number of other people and turn them into Don Quixotes about whom they write and sing songs. The cautious and deliberate among us, the 'let's think this all through now' types aren't the kind they write books or ballads about. We couldn't be tamer or more boring. When the U.K. was about to explode its first hydrogen bomb in the pacific, the churches wrung their hands and had emergency meetings but a quiet little preacher, sixty-years of age, withdrew all his savings, bought a boat and sailed right into the area. After dealing with the inconvenience Britain went on to make its nuclear test. The little man accomplished nothing, we say. Oh, I don't know. He still tugs at our conscience more than forty years later.

Meanwhile, the good news is that 'Captain Freedom' is alive and well in the persons of those who renounce all the warring ways to bring peace, all the evil ways to make society better, all the filthy ways to make us clean and all the enslaving ways to make us free. So here's to you who continue the battle against evil, even when you are not convinced that your little gesture will make much difference. Here's to you who lay your reputations on the line, risking the sniggers and put-downs. Here's to you who confront evil, taking it on with no weapons other than those with which Jesus Christ faced His 'Judgement at Golgotha'. Let them snigger and say you're a fool. Long after 'what's his name' has been fully forgotten someone will speak your name in grudging admiration. Sad Matthew Arnold wrote this inspiring thing:

Creep into thy narrow bed
Creep, and let no more be said!
Vain thy onset! All stands fast.
Thou thyself must break at last.

Let the long contentions cease!
Geese are swans and swans are geese.
Let them have it how they will!
Thou art tired; best be still.

They out-talk'd thee, hissed thee, tore thee?
Better men have fared thus before thee;
Fired their ringing shot and pass'd,
Hotly charged—and sank at last.

Charge once more, then, and be dumb!
Let the victors when they come,
When the forts of folly fall,
Find thy body by the wall.

ELEVEN

'Robert, I'd like to speak to you for a moment, in private, if I may'

I know it's a terrible thing to confess, but it's true. I have some dear friends I don't want to share with others. Well, that's not quite what I'm wanting to say. I'm glad they have other friends but I don't want them to be as special to them as they are to me. To think that they feel toward others as deeply as they feel toward me, seems to diminish me, to take something from me. I know it's nonsense. More than that, I know it's selfish of me and in my better moments I renounce it for what it is but there is that character flaw in me that results in my wanting to monopolise their warmth and intimacy. I'm afraid they might care for others in such a way that I lose a special place in their lives, don't you see. I'm sure there's something of that spirit in my relationship with God even though I know He's capable of loving everyone without anyone losing out. Just the same, sometimes, when things are a little harder to handle than usual, I can't help feeling that since I'm God's child that should mean I get special treatment. I mean 'special' in the pleasant sense.

It's hard for us 'decent people' (which often includes non-Christians) to understand why we don't get privileged treatment from God. Rather than my offering you a list of 'explanations' let me share something that helped me to understand my feelings better and that made me willing to think the thing through more patiently. In the movie, *Glory*, the son of a wealthy and prominent abolitionist is commissioned to head-up the first black regiment of the Union army. His first volunteer is, Thomas, his life-long friend. Thomas is free, well educated, well-spoken, refined and well thought of but when he enlists he becomes a private and his life-long friend becomes his superior officer. Because they've enjoyed this wonderful relationship down the years, Thomas can't help but expect special treatment—instead he finds himself isolated from his friend. Private moments cease completely, personal conversation no longer exists and all tokens of affection are gone.

The master-sergeant is giving Thomas an especially tough time precisely because he is the colonel's dear friend and the colonel is having to endure it even though it's breaking his heart. In one scene, the master-sergeant has again humiliated and injured Thomas and later when the sensitive young black man sobbingly pleads, 'Robert, I'd like to speak to you for a moment in private, if I may,' the colonel reminds him that he must go through channels if he is to speak to his superior officer. 'Do you understand that, private?' he asks, and then walks away. From a place of warm privilege where he was known to and loved by his friend and his family, Thomas is non-brutally but decisively pushed back into the mass of other black volunteers. The other soldiers, dirt-poor and strangers to comforts had never known such privilege and so didn't miss the smiles, the warmth, the hugs, the moments of shared privacy. For Thomas the special relationship is now a source of awful pain. Surely the colonel can't treat him as though he had never known him? What harm can be done by maintaining their beautiful, warm friendship? How can he pretend that Thomas is no different than all these strangers? And so his pain is worse than the pain of all those who never had Colonel Robert G. Shaw as a friend. Thomas' pain was not due to the fact that the colonel was making a difference between him and the other troops, it was because he *wasn't* making a difference—that's what devastated Thomas. But as the story unfolds, Thomas comes to terms with what he knows in his heart needs to be done and so he sorrowfully surrenders his intimacy with the colonel for the welfare of all the other volunteers with whom he now develops a new sense of brotherhood. The early Thomas was noble and honourable; the later Thomas was even nobler.

Perhaps we should recognise that there's more at stake than our getting special treatment from a God who is our friend. It might be important that we *don't* get special treatment. However hard it might be for us to step back and take our place along with all the other 'enlisted' people who don't feel they are owed special treatment, Thomas calls us to that. If our Friend will not exempt us from agony, not allow us to go to his tent for a private talk anytime we wish, we may feel more than hurt—we may feel abandoned! If only, as Job and Thomas pleaded, we could have a moment in private where we could make our Friend see

He was overdoing it all a little, that He should ease the situation, not much, just enough to make it more bearable. (For all the blessing which comes from prayer, each sensitive person knows there are times when God remains silent and aloof.)

So brave, sorrowful Thomas finally bites the bullet, endures the agony and becomes a hero. On Christmas-eve night, the colonel is walking between the tents, alone and feeling lonely. He and Thomas meet by accident—both lonely and in awful pain. The black man, speaking with difficulty says, 'Robert, I just wanted to say...I just wanted to say...' and then, unable to finish what he started and with a sad little smile, he just gently says, 'Merry Christmas, Robert.'

Maybe while there is a child anywhere in the world who is subjected to pain, maybe while there is a man or woman anywhere in the world who has to wrestle with humiliation, hunger and injustice that leaves them speechless, maybe as long as any of that goes on we won't get special treatment. While any of that is going on maybe we shouldn't want special treatment. Maybe that's something of what the incarnation and Gethsemane's 'nevertheless' mean. Maybe that's what, 'Eloi, Eloi, Lama Sabacthani?' means. Maybe there are times when we're about to pour out a string of requests to a God we think should give us preferential treatment—maybe we should forget the list and tell Him, 'Merry Christmas, Father!'

SECTION THREE:
CLEARER VISION

ONE

The struggler's need of clear vision

One of the finest gifts we can share with strugglers is clear vision.

Much of the pain we experience in life, much of the pain we inflict on others is the result of pathetic vision.

We want to avoid pain, don't you see, and so we're blind to the benefits (for ourselves and others) that can come from having to endure pain. We enjoy the blessings of life and can't see we're becoming obsessed with them. We see ourselves as paragons of virtue and lose touch with basic courtesy. We fear the future and lose the possibility of joy now as a result of that fear. We get caught up in all kinds of 'good works' and become shallow and virtually powerless because we do nothing well. We gorge ourselves on the demands of our passions and miss the joy and satisfaction of things which go deeper. We experience a new sensitivity to our selfishness and become addicted to misery. And so on.

Those people do us a great service who teach us to see the broader picture. They help us to balance our judgements, to engage in healthy self-examination and develop the ability to see the issues of life as a wise order of importance.

Harry Emerson Fosdick liked to say there are two ways of looking at the cross of Christ. You can look at the cross itself, see it for what it is, a stark witness to the incredible evil in the world *and* as a consequence, say, 'How can there be a good God with this in the world?' On the other hand, you can look at the Christ on the cross and ask, 'How can there *not* be a good God with Him in the world?' This has stuck with me down the years and reminded me that there is more than one way to look at things. Clearer vision is a precious gift indeed.

TWO

Silverware and toothpicks

It happened on a flight from Bangkok to Singapore on Cathay Pacific Airlines. They brought the dinners round and while I can't remember what it was, I remember that I thought it was absolutely marvellous. The food was great but the silverware was beautiful—the kind you'd expect to come across in a four-star, swanky hotel. (As it turned out, I wasn't the only one impressed by the cutlery.) I had that nice contented feeling as I looked round at my fellow-travellers and my eye settled on a gentleman just in front of me across the aisle. He was using a toothpick but he was covering what he was doing with his hand (this is good manners in that part of the world). I'd been told of this practice but it was the first time I had actually noticed it and I was thinking how polite it all was. He wiped his very attractive silverware clean, looked around and promptly stuffed it into his little attache case. *He was stealing the silverware!* I couldn't help smiling. Truth is, I nearly burst out laughing, at a man who was so careful about the practice of good manners but who then proceeded to rob the airline.

And I recalled an illustration used by Jesus Christ in the Bible. It wasn't unusual in His part of the world for religious men to put a piece of fine cloth over the mouth of the water-skin so that when they drank they would not be ceremonially defiled by swallowing a little fly which had got into the water. But while they were so fussy about the minor issues of life, they dismissed and left undone the more important matters of life, like justice, mercy and faithfulness (Matthew 23:23). Jesus described this kind of person as one who 'strained out tiny flies but swallowed camels' (camels were ceremonially unclean animals).

It's another mark of our wretchedness that we choose to obey what suits us and transgress what doesn't. We have laws against marijuana but live contentedly with the damnable booze industry. We teach the mechanics of sex to children without giving it any spiritual dimension and shake our heads at the rising figures on teenage pregnancies, abortions and disease. We commit murder but protest the death penalty as uncivilised and we rape, plunder, maim and murder our children while we save the whale or some other lovely creature. We exasperate people to the point of madness and then ask them to act reasonably, we scream sectarian and nationalistic hatred for decades and then act as though we are amazed when a new and sinister breed of politician arises. (You see this with special clarity here in Northern Ireland.)

Church-going people are not exempt from all this, in fact, the words of Jesus Christ were addressed to God-fearing people. We cluck our tongues over the crazy hair styles and dress of the young and slander fellow-believers; we are stunned by the foul speech we hear on television and on street corners while we speak foul slander or soul-withering gossip. We spend much of our time dealing with trivial biblical questions while vast issues and global needs stare us in the face. We vehemently denounce sectarian violence but cannot have peace in our own assemblies. We leave our religious fortresses every now and then to carry back to them someone who was 'in the world'; someone we now isolate from the world (as we have isolated ourselves) and then damn the world in our sermons because they are going deeper and deeper into moral and spiritual decline. We take 'out of' the world the very people who should be allowed to permeate the world and at the same time expect (so we say) the world to get better. Amazing!

I used to think we were very different from the world in general but, in general, I'm not now convinced of that at all. Of course, I know a great number of Christians whose lives are noble and winsome but I know a great number of non-Christians whose lives are just as gallant and lovely. (Thank God, God doesn't work only in the lives of the church-going.) It's absolutely imperative that we oppose evil within us and around us and that we seek to embody and proclaim an ethic derived from the Bible but I'm certain that we need to humbly re-examine our priorities and practise. We need clearer vision, we need to have a better idea of what we're here for, what's important, more important and most important.

THREE

The reward of integrity

The Bible tells the story of Jacob. As a young man he had taken advantage of his twin brother and extorted from him the major share of the family inheritance. A little while later he fooled his aged father, cheated the brother out of further blessing and then fled the country. Now, twenty years later, he must return to face his twin which has him scared witless. Had Jacob been upright he wouldn't have been worried sick. It's true, 'Conscience doth make cowards of us all.'

Our mouths go dry, our pulse hammers in our throat just at the thought of our shame being discovered. We imagine people are talking about us, snubbing us, avoiding us. A letter not answered or a phone call not returned torments us with the thought that our 'secret' is known. The pain we endure as a result of our lack of honour so far outweighs any pleasure dishonour brings that it's a wonder any of us stoops to being treacherous.

The young man tried to talk the young lady into sexual intercourse but she wouldn't hear tell of it. Then he offered her booze she wouldn't touch. A little later he wanted to share some marijuana with her but she turned that down too. By this time he was thoroughly disgusted and sulkily demanded to know what she did for fun. She said:

'I never have to worry about being diseased or pregnant. And that's fun! That means I don't have to wrestle with a decision to abort an unwanted baby; and that's fun. And I don't have to wonder if I'm being pawed over by someone who might not want to know me a couple of months from now. And that's fun. I never have any difficulty remembering what I did the night before and who I did it with; and that's fun too. And I'm looking forward to the day when I can give myself totally to my husband rather than give a panicky fraction of me in the back seat of some car. And that's fun. I can hardly wait, but I will. I won't ever have to worry about getting a blood test that tells me I have AIDS or some other venereal disease; and believe me, that's fun. My parents love me more than I can say and if I were to get into trouble, of any kind, they'd be right there with me. But I never have to worry about seeing them crushed and shamed by some disgraceful behaviour of mine, and believe me, as much as I love them—that's really fun.'

I've taken a beating when I was innocent and I've taken a beating when I was guilty and I can tell you, there's no fun in being beaten when you've asked for it. At least when you're innocent in the matter, you can always go away from the beating with the inner comfort that this time, if the truth were known, you suffered in innocence. And that, even in the midst of pain, is fun!

FOUR

We'd let Him in wouldn't we?

It was 11 July, 1971—a very good year. In Northern Ireland that week of July means flute bands, processions of marchers thousands strong, 'Union Jack' flags everywhere, kerbstones painted red, white and blue, streets decorated with mock city walls, streamers and wall paintings, dancing in the streets, bonfires at every other intersection if the buildings are thought to be able to stand the terrific heat (some buildings are covered and hosed down throughout the night). And there is booze, yes, plenty of booze and pubs packed to the doors. This is the time when the Protestant/Unionists celebrate an ancient victory over the Nationalist/Catholic forces. One of the thousands of marchers in the 'Orange Order' was Johnny Martin who each year carried the symbolic sabre as he marched triumphantly to 'the Field' where the multitude, weary with the march, would gladly sit and listen to a series of speakers calling them to 'maintain the Union'—with Britain. Johnny was a painter by trade and a hard drinker by habit.

I came on the scene when Johnny's wife Peggy was very ill with a cancer which would brutally and swiftly rob her of life at the age of thirty-eight, forcing her to leave behind a daughter (Ethel) and two sons (Jackie and Roy). Later he would remarry and he and his devoted wife, Helen, would have a boy, Paul. When his daughter and her daughter (Linda) went to see the bonfire at 'the Nick', Johnny had already been drunk and sober several times that 11th day of July. Up the street he came, well into another binge, extra whiskey in his pockets and plenty of time to get it down him. He tried to cuddle his six-year-old granddaughter but she began to cry big tears and to tell him she didn't like the way he smelled. That broke his heart and then and there he swore to her that he would never drink again. That very night he gave his life to Christ, the booze was dumped and Johnny Martin hasn't had a drop in over twenty years. Marvellous! This kind of turn around is by no means rare but it's remarkable just the same.

It's funny how many things God uses in his attempts to turn us around. Even the things which God doesn't actively bring our way (things like the birth of a baby suffering from spina bifida), can be used to touch our hearts. A tragic event, a lovely book, a splendid movie, the patience of a wife, the suffering of innocent children, a close brush with death, the loyalty of a friend, the strength and gentleness of a physically big man. Six-year-old Linda's tears tugged on Johnny Martin's heart strings.

He had taken his little girl to an art gallery, so the story went. She showed no interest at all until they came to a picture of a tired looking man, knocking and knocking on a door. The picture showed people on the other side of the door—it looked like they had no plans to open it. She was hooked. 'Who is that?' she asked her dad. How could she know the question would trouble his heart; the heart of a man who was wrestling with deep questions. 'It's Jesus,' he heard himself say with a slight edge to his voice. A pause, and then, 'Won't they let him in?' Unease was beginning to grow in the man but he could hardly brush her off so he quietly said, 'No they won't let him in.' Quick as light she asked, 'Is he bad?' and he shot back just as fast, 'No! He isn't bad.' Faster still, she demanded, 'Well, then, why won't they let him in?' Now he's really uneasy, he's had enough and as he gently but firmly walks her away from the picture he hears himself say in a tone too terse, 'How do I know?' She senses the tension and says no more but every now and then big, dark, round eyes glance at him and then in the direction of the portrait. She knows he knows something he won't tell her.

At supper no word was said about it but the eyes kept talking. After supper she got ready for bed, pyjamas on, teeth brushed and with toothpaste still around her mouth she climbed up on his lap and hugged his neck longer than usual. Then she kissed him, headed for the bedroom, stopped, turned and said, 'We'd let him in, wouldn't we!' Then off she went to sleep like a log while all through the grown man's sleepless night God was prying his heart open with a child's words. I'm told that just like my father-in-law, Johnny Martin, the Man 'let him in'.

Gone 'Home'

A religion which plays down life and relationships here and now is not of God! That kind of religion only undermines the glory and worth of loving marriages, family relationships and noble friendships. It kills enthusiasm for social involvement and community cooperation by promoting a 'pie-in-the-sky-by-and-by' mentality; a 'nothing down here is worth bothering with' attitude. This is not the religion of the 'incarnate God' who lovingly created our world and then entered it in Jesus Christ!

But it is equally unacceptable to look at humans and sum them up as a 'curious accident in a cosmic backwater'. There are drives and hungers in thoughtful people which aren't satisfied by satisfying the needs of the body. It isn't only Christians who feel that man can't *live* by bread alone. You can see it in the graffiti on Belfast walls. 'We don't want bread, we want justice!' I watched him on television. He was dying of cancer in a hospice. An articulate man in his sixties who, when asked, said, 'Oh, I believe we're just like washing-machines. We have our circuitry and programmes and when we wear out that's the end of us.' Then a glance at the floor, a long look at the interviewer, and an intense addition, 'But I pray every day without fail.' The most serious objection to atheistic humanism? H. J. Blackham, the humanist said, 'It's the pointlessness of it all...It's too bad to be true.' Food, clothes, housing, music, education, athletic success, wealth in abundance—marvellous things but.... just... not....enough. There's something else! Something more!

E.T. is a little alien in a Spielberg movie. He was left stranded on earth but was befriended by some children who gave him shelter, protection and affection. They taught him the word 'home' and asked him where his 'home' is. He conjures up a celestial model to explain and later waddles to the window, points out into the night sky with a long finger and mournfully says, 'Home.' The children offer him all they have and it was a lot! It was warm and loving and genuine but it wasn't enough. Within him was a hunger and a loneliness which couldn't be satisfied on earth and several times throughout the movie we hear that heart-wrenching sound, 'Home'.

You should enjoy the blessings of life here (they're God's gifts to you!) and you *should* hold life on earth as dear but don't demand of it more than they can give. In those periods of your life when you feel that emptiness we all feel from time to time, don't deny it or suppress it—pay attention to it. It's God's way of telling you you were made for more. Don't dismiss the wistfulness, let it have its way for a while. Learn from it, don't be afraid or ashamed of it. Let it bring its message and when that health-bringing discontent nibbles at the edges of your mind, look upward and think 'Home.'

Gyp the preacher

Pericles was one of ancient Greece's greatest orators as well as one of its greatest statesmen. I've read that he refused to speak more than two or three times a year in the senate even though he attended regularly and everyone entreated him to do so when he was there. He thought that making too many speeches hurt a man and hurt his hearers and hurt the noble causes that they all espoused. So he didn't speak very often and, as a consequence, when he did it had a real impact. The principles involved here apply to more than making speeches or preaching sermons.

John Broadbank, said Frank Boreham, hadn't learned to say *no*! He got involved in every project he came across and spoke at every conference he was invited to. The more he travelled, the greater grew his fame and the greater the fame, the more they invited him on to their boards and conference platforms. His family suffered loss in all this and one day his devoted wife sobbed out to him how lonely she was and how guilty she felt for feeling that way. A week at home without a project made him realise how much of a whirl his life had become. It was about that time that he came across *Gyp*.

He was walking across a field when he saw a man down by a pond drowning a terrier dog. Broadbank asked him why, and the man said, 'Well, you see, sir, when he was a pup he was all right and we were fond of him. We called him "Gypsy"—*Gyp* for short. But now he's become to be a regular nuisance. We're always losing him. He follows everybody and the dog that follows everybody is no good to anybody.' *The dog that follows everybody is no good to anybody!* He pleaded with the man to give him the dog; which he did. John walked off with the terrier. 'Come on Gyp,' he said, 'I've been a bit of a gypsy myself. You and I will teach each other better manners.'

But it's more than a question of better manners, isn't it? It becomes a question of fruitfulness and sometimes a question of character. It may be tempting to believe your own 'press' and think the world of speeches, sermons, noble causes and community projects would be utterly impoverished without you (if they could survive at all). It's a mistake to spread yourself too thin. As John Broadbank finally admitted, '*On the whole, it's better to be narrow and deep.*' I was amazed (and pleased) to read a few years ago Billy Graham was quoted as saying, if he had it all to do again he would 'speak less and study more'. Imagine that, coming from a man who has probably addressed more people than any other religious man in history.

Teaching, like character, if it's to be rich and fruitful, has to put down deep roots. 'Nibbling on the run,' in the end, destroys the effectiveness and fruitfulness of a speaker. It robs others too. The speeches begin to bristle with clichés, one-liners and well-worn stories which grow more wonderful with the telling. People go away no longer impressed with the 'flair' or 'talk'— and sorely hunger for something substantial or at least sorely need even if they don't hunger for it. They begin to realise as J. S. Stewart, put it, that 'the Lord was not in the wind.'

Wouldn't it be sad if Christ, asking where we were, said, 'I can't say, I keep losing him. He follows everyone you know.'

SEVEN

Smoke and smugness

We went to Furr's cafeteria. There were about eight or nine of us. All dedicated preachers of Christ. We were going to discuss better ways and means to reach the unforgiven of earth with the saving message of Jesus Christ. Since none of us smoke we found seats in the section marked, 'Reserved for non-smokers'. Not long after we began our fervent discussion about the saving of the unforgiven, three ladies (or was it four?) sat down at the table next to ours. At least one of them lit up a cigarette and contentedly puffed away.

The smoke and the smell reached our dedicated little group. Up went the heads, sniff went the noses and then the muttering began. The murmur increased to a low-key protest at the nerve of the woman who was infringing on our rights. We had our rights! we told one another. I don't like cigarette smoke. It irritates me as it swirls around me, subjecting me to its cancer-provoking properties. (I know about smoking from both sides since I used to irritate people and contaminate them during my long affair with 'the weed'.)

I was closest to her. And above the rising din of

protesting indignant men the lady caught *my* words. I don't remember what they were. Some remark or other about people taking other people's rights away by smoking in a clearly marked non-smoking area. She turned to me immediately and humbly apologised. She said, 'I'm very sorry. I didn't know this was a non-smoking section.' She extinguished her cigarette and returned to visiting with her friends.

I was too embarrassed by her genuine apology to say anything in return. I should have resisted that and apologised to her. *She* had acted in a Christian manner. Instead of our muttering against the lady we should have gently asked her if she was aware that she was in a non-smoking section. That is, if we had felt the need of insisting on our rights. I don't remember much of what was said in the next hour. I was thinking of the reason for our gathering. I was wondering what chance the unforgiven had if those who went preaching went as we were. As I was.

I'm still amazed at times at my smugness and at the utter inconsistency and incompatibility between the attitude I showed there and my stated desire. Whatever would happen to the rest of the world. There was a lady right there next to us who didn't even receive as much as a kind word from any of us. It amazed me that I was virtually saying to that woman that she would have to act as suited me if she expected me to reflect Christ before her. I'm amazed that we were going to send young men and women out into the world to adjust, submit, give up rights, say good-bye to comforts and pleasures in order to manifest Christ, verbally and vitally, while we couldn't endure a lady encroaching on our space. God help us. God forgive us! God deliver us from delivering implicit ultimatums such as: Make yourself acceptable to me and I'll share Christ with you. God give us a clearer vision of ourselves and redeem us from becoming or remaining pompous asses.

EIGHT

Did you forget the candlesticks?

He was twenty-seven, a hard-working and illiterate peasant who picked fruit for a living. He lived with his sister and her seven children and while the pay was pathetic, it was a job. Winter came, he had no work and the family had literally nothing to eat. He endured their pain until he could endure it no longer and that's what led him to break the window of a baker's shop and steal a loaf. He was spotted! In the chase he threw the loaf away but the cut on his arm proved his guilt and the court gave him five years hard labour. He pleaded and protested (five years hard labour for stealing a loaf?) but it made no difference and in chains, with a metal collar around his neck they carted him off to slavery. In days when despair overwhelmed him his fellow-prisoners would see his lips move soundlessly while he wept and they'd see his raised right hand drop in stages as though he were laying his hand on heads of unequal height. For the children! He did it for the children. A loaf, for pity's sake—it was only a loaf!

Four times he tried to escape but he only succeeded in adding years to his term. When they set him free he had served nineteen years. Nineteen years to harbour deep bitterness, nineteen years to feed his anger, nineteen years— long enough to be dehumanised, to want to vent his spite against all around him, to hate and expect to be hated.

They gave him a yellow card which he had to show to law-abiding citizens. It meant he was a convict, newly released, on probation and on his way to a town chosen for him by the authorities. When he came to the town in which Bienvenu Myriel lived, the former convict was rejected by the inn-keepers despite his willingness to pay his way for food and lodging. Not a barn was open to him. He was even driven from a kennel by a huge dog and he found himself trying to sleep in the open, in the rain, on a wooden bench. Nineteen years serving in prison and on the galleys and now this! 'Have you knocked on that door?' a kind lady asked him. No he hadn't but he would, and did.

The door was opened and before anyone could reject him, the miserable and desperate man thundered out his name and the fact that he was a convict. He almost challenged anyone to reject his pleading for food and rest unaware that he had come to the house of a bishop. The bishop who lived in utter simplicity, without grandeur or luxury, invited him in by the fire, urged the ladies to make him welcome and set the table for supper. The visitor suddenly realised he was dealing with a priest. 'Ah, you're a priest. I saw a bishop once...' he babbled on and described the fine clothing of the bishop. The old man kept calling him 'mister' in that respectful way and Jean (John) Valjean was warmed by this new treatment.

Supper (a simple but substantial meal) was served on silver plates and Valjean ate his fill. The ladies retired to bed, the old man went to pray and meditate and the exhausted visitor collapsed on the warm bed to sleep. A good while before dawn the convict entered the old man's room prepared to injure or kill him and steal the silver cutlery and plates. The sight of the trustful priest in peaceful sleep kept Valjean from the mad violence but he gathered the silver together, climbed the garden wall and went his way.

The next morning the theft was discovered and a little later three policemen dragged the ex-convict before the priest. They addressed the old man as 'Monseigneur' and 'his lordship the Bishop'. The stupefied Valjean heard the old man say to him: 'So here you are! I'm delighted to see you. Had you forgotten that I gave you the candlesticks as well? They're silver like the rest, and worth a good two hundred francs. Did you forget to take them?' The astonished policemen left and the bishop, gently and deliberately, said to Valjean, 'Jean Valjean my brother, you no longer belong to what is evil but to what is good. I have bought your soul to save it from black perdition, and I give it to God.'

You recognize, of course, the story-line of the incredible *Les Miserables* by Victor Hugo. I love the compassion of the old bishop and the consequent transformation of the brutal ex-convict into a man of tenderness, compassion and selflessness. In this story, as so often in life itself, this kind compassion turned the world of the wrongdoer upside down; it wouldn't let him continue as he was; it melted his icy heart and gave him inspiration and strength to live a redemptive life and to make life better and stronger for

111

others battling against the darkness that threatens to swallow them up. From that point on, the candlesticks were kept in a prominent place and became the symbol of the compassion shown to Valjean and the voiceless reminder of the debt he owed to all other fellow-strugglers.

To do what is right and kind and brave is what God calls us to. This we should do no matter what the results. But there's no way of knowing how such behaviour alters the world for a person who is badly in need of such a vision. When a life has been filled with pain and injustice, with brutality and callousness, darkness invades the soul. It becomes difficult or almost impossible for the heart to believe there is any other reality. The old bishop's incredible kindness stood up and, in the name of God, defied the supremacy of darkness and Valjean's world changed, his eyes were opened never to be closed. He now possessed a new vision which he couldn't deny.

NINE

Benjamin

A little boy came to me one day and told me he had got in to trouble with the principal at school. I asked for the details—it was the kind of trouble a twelve-year-old boy gets into. He was afraid of his father hearing about it, afraid the principal would call him and tell him about it and what on earth would the boy do if that happened? He said— with the intensity that only a boy is capable of in situations like this—he thought that if he had a gun he could kill himself. Yes! I put my arm around my son, George, and assured him that he could never get in to such trouble that I'd want him to do anything like that. When he was gone, a great sadness filled me. What kind of a world is it, what kind of a life is it that people like me are making when a little boy with wide and tear-filled eyes could speak with such intensity about killing himself over boyish mistakes which might make their way to his father? Worry is the gnawing fear we experience in the face of possible loss and the loss is usually a major one. There are so many things to worry about, aren't there? I'm not so dumb as not to know there are things serious enough to make us worry. I chafe a little to hear isolated Bible verses about worry, used to add deep guilt feelings to those who are worried over some very serious situation that has arisen in their lives. Pounding the pulpit and berating people who worry isn't only poor use of the Bible, it only gives the worrier something more to worry about. But we need to do something to help people to put things in perspective. We need a new vision. Another way of looking at things. Even death itself.

Young Benjamin, so the story goes, was 'awfully fearful of dying'. It seems he was terminally ill and, in the way that children do, he picked up on what he wasn't supposed to pick up on. One day as he walked in the garden, feeling anxious, a voice said, 'What's wrong with you, Benjamin?' And when he looked it was a flower. When he had recovered from the shock of learning that flowers talk, he said he was terribly afraid of dying. At this the flower laughed and said, 'You're silly. I love to die. I get to feeling droopy and weary and then I die and wake up all fresh and new.' Benjamin wanted to share the laughter but the only thing he could come up with was, 'Well, that's all right for you. You're a flower and I'm a boy.'

On another day as he lay under a tree feeling poorly and worrying about what would happen, a tiny voice asked him what was bothering him. This time it was a caterpillar. By now the boy realised that all kinds of things talked if only people would hear them. 'I'm awfully fearful of dying' he said and the caterpillar rolled all over the place, laughing, like a tiny ringing bell. 'You're *afraid* of dying?' he tittered as he hung upside down from a plant, 'I *love* to die. I just wrap up in my covering and when I wake up I'm all changed and beautiful. I can fly and everything. Dying is nothing to be afraid of!' The boy wanted to feel that way, to believe that story but, again, all he could do was murmur, 'It's different with little boys,' and he walked back into the house, still worried about dying.

One day he was feeling very tired indeed, the sun was hurting his eyes and he felt he just had to lie down; and he did. He fell into a deep sleep and when he awoke, somehow he felt better though still he was worried as he walked out into the garden. He met an angel there. Though he had never seen an angel before, somehow he just knew this was an angel who gently asked him, 'Benjamin, what's troubling you?' and the boy said, 'I'm awfullly fearful of dying.' The angel smiled and said, 'Why, Benjamin, you *are* dead!' This sad little boy did all that worrying and then one day he just up and did it and discovered it wasn't so bad after all.

Many people fear a prolonged and painful illness before death. They not only fear it because they have a healthy dislike for pain, they fear it for their family. The trauma, the helplessness, and, in some countries, the staggering cost of medical care. All this makes sense though there isn't much that can be done about it. People must do what they can to get ready emotionally and spiritually before the day arrives.

Suffering may not come but death certainly will and there's a definite approach we can make to that. It's enough that we have grounds for concern about suffering before 'going away'. We need to enjoy the comfort of our faith about death itself. 'If we believe that Jesus Christ died and rose again,' said a tremendous sufferer and martyr, we know that our loved ones who have died in Him are safe and well! And it's because people have found Jesus Christ, who experienced death for all of us, that people have found Him persuasive and we find things like this written on grave-stones:

Gone Away With A Friend.

Another one reads like this:

Freddie! Yes, Father!

John Donne's magnificent poem, *Death Be Not Proud*, calls us to a trustful defiance and so does the way a group of Christians in ancient Smyrna marked their calendar. Polycarp, their old and much loved leader had calmly refused to choose life if it meant spurning Jesus Christ, so he cheerfully chose death in the fire. The young church at Smyrna recorded the event this way, 'Polycarp was mar-tyred, Statius Quadratus being proconsul of Asia, and Jesus Christ being King for ever.' Death is over-rated. If even half of what we sing is true, if even half of what we pray is true, if any of the central truths we have learned about Jesus Christ are true, Death is over-rated! As Donne would put it:

One short sleep past, we wake eternally,
And Death shall be no more:
Death, thou shalt die!

TEN

Pale Galilean

The poet Swinburne blamed Jesus for taking the zest out of life. He said, 'Thou hast conquered, pale Galilean; all the world grows grey at thy breath.' Let's face it, Swinburne didn't learn this from Jesus. He learned it from Christ's followers. Non-Christians are often full-blooded while many saints are anaemic. Lots of people, before they come to Christ, are full of life and a joy to be around. Then they come to Christ and become joyless and miserable. Lots of children find that God 'stole' their good-natured and joyful father and turned him into a grim, stern and joyless man who has no time for living. What do you think these children will think of God?

Wives find their husbands transformed into tight-lipped, spiritual nags who have lost their ability to laugh or spend carefree time with them or the children. Husbands have discovered that Jesus didn't make their wives happier, they have become tight as banjo strings and seem to have a permanent case of the 'blahs'. Friends have lost friends 'to the Church' and have been unable to find them again. It isn't just that their former friends won't engage in objectionable behaviour, they've lost their capacity for laughter, fun, appreciation for the ordinary things of life. No wonder poor Swinburne missed the mark completely. The friends, representatives and companions of Christ are so often dull, drab, joyless and grim so Swinburne blamed Christ. Some saints can't enjoy a meal because the world is starving. They can't joyfully thank God for their clothing and shelter because the world is naked and homeless. They are afraid to smile because of the world's sadness. They're afraid to enjoy salvation because of the world's lost ones. They can't enjoy an evening at home with their families because they feel they ought to be out 'saving souls'. They can't spend an hour with an unforgiven one without feeling guilty if they haven't preached a sermon or manifested a 'sober Christian spirit'. They know nothing of balance. And they're miserable because of it. They have no inner incentive to bring people into a relationship with Christ which would make them feel as miserable as they themselves feel. They think the Gospel is 'good news' until you obey it and then it becomes an endless guilt-trip.

It often gets to the point where they can't even accept that they're 'ordinary' sinners. They feel obliged to exaggerate even that and so are in need of this rebuke:

Once in a saintly passion
I cried in bitter grief,
O Lord, my heart is filled with guile
Of sinners I'm the chief;
Then stooped my guardian angel
And whispered from behind,
'Vanity my little man,
You're nothing of the kind'.

118

There are leisure centres, sports centres, sewing centres, diet centres, entertainment centres and guilt centres. This last group is usually called 'Churches'. The endless harping on the string of guilt is part of the reason for all this gloom and uncertainty. Preachers usually *quote* scriptures on joy and *expound* scriptures on guilt. There's little sense in asking people share what is bringing them only pain.

Relax! Enjoy the Master and as you pursue his likeness you'll find yourself caring and sharing. In the meantime, let it be known that you're Christ's and let people know that Jesus doesn't hurt marriages or injure family ties. He doesn't make people sour and He doesn't steal your friends. He insists that people surrender themselves to Him and then they learn to live as they've never known. They get that joyous approach to life that an eighty-five-year-old only discovered when he learned he was dying of cancer. In the letter which made it's way into a psychology journal, the old man said:

> If I had my life to live over again, I'd try to make more next time. I wouldn't try to be so perfect. I'd relax more.
>
> I'd limber up. I'd be sillier than I've been on this trip. In fact, I know very few things that I would take so seriously.
>
> I'd be crazier. I'd be less hygienic. I'd take more chances, I'd take more trips, I'd climb more mountains, I'd swim more rivers, I'd watch more sunsets, I'd go more places I've never been to. I'd eat more ice-cream and fewer beans. I'd play

hookey from school more often. I'd have more actual troubles and fewer imaginary ones.

...I've been one of those people who never went anywhere without a thermometer, a hot water bottle, a gargle, a raincoat, and a parachute. If I had to do it all over again, I'd travel lighter next time. I'd start barefoot earlier in the spring and stay that way later in the fall. I'd ride more merry-go-rounds, I'd watch more sunrises, I'd kiss more children and I'd tell more people that I love them; if I had my life to live over again but you see, I don't.

ELEVEN

You can trust Albert

My favourite story about Mrs Einstein happened when reporters were asking her if she understood Albert's big words. She said she understood a lot of them, one at a time; it was when he put them together in sentences that things got tough. Then they asked her if she understood his two theories of relativity. She said, 'No...but you can trust Albert!' Don't you love that? She couldn't understand the jargon or the deeper doctrines but she knew the man. The formulas and equations had her beat but on the relational kind of truth she was the world's leading authority.

It's perfectly legitimate (and unavoidable) to describe life and living realities in words and phrases (as far as that is possible) but often those who define them best understand them least and those who define them most poorly know them best! This is verified when you meet up with people who profess no religious faith but whose lives are noble and gallant as distinct from those who can rehearse, word-perfect, their religious creed or reams of scriptures from the Bible but whose lives are narrow, joyless, trivial or self-righteous (or any one or combination of these).

There's a mental disorder (I've forgotten its Latin

name) which affects the poor victim like this. He pores over maps, memorises places, rivers, roads, points of departure and points of arrival, mountains and valleys and the like. And then, in his confusion, he thinks he has made the trip.

A specialist in the religious manifestation of this disorder describes it like this, 'The peril of religion is that vital experience shall be resolved into a formula of explanation, and that men, grasping the formula, shall suppose themselves thereby to possess the experience.'

Howard Butt tells us that back in 1950 some young people discovered a gold mine in New York. It was during the peak months when South Pacific was playing on Broadway. Rodgers and Hammerstein's blockbuster was enjoying sellout crowds while the European heart-throb, Ezio Pinza, was singing to America's sweetheart Mary Martin. They came from every little town in the country to see the show but they hadn't a hope. Tickets were non existent. The young New Yorkers picked up or bought used ticket-stubs or programmes around the theatre and sold them to rural Americans who didn't like to go home confessing they hadn't seen the show. Back home in 'the sticks' with programmes, ticket stubs and humming a few well rehearsed bars of *Some Enchanted Evening* the big-timers made their friends jealous. They had everything—everything but the experience!

Second-hand religion is a poor substitute for the real thing. But, then, so is second-hand living. To allow society to pour you into its own mould is as bad for non-Christians as it is for Christians. A few beers, a couple of weeks in Spain each year, hours of television each day and a 'lie in' on Sunday morning is hardly living. A dusty Bible, church attendance a couple of times a week and copious tears over the documentary which shows the exploitation and rape of millions isn't much better.

It's as sad a spectacle to see religious people with their 'hearsay' religion berate the 'unbelievers' as it is to see 'unbelievers' with their 'borrowed' philosophy, tired old arguments against God's existence and anti-church feeling berate the church-goers. While they're hammering each other, life is slipping by and noble causes with eternal consequences are left unsupported by both camps. Speaking as one Christian, I believe we're all going to meet God and, wherever we stood on 'formulas', we're going to answer for not having some genuine 'experience' of life if that's how it is with us.

TWELVE

The Key

I'm one of those who enjoys reading. I don't know how many books I read a year but it's a considerable number and although most of it's non-fiction I do read what I judge to be good fiction. Ethel and I both enjoy movies and we try to watch them together. You know, movies 'like they used to make them'. The old black and white ones, where you knew who the bad guys were and the good guys always won. I know of tough 'realists' who are glad that that kind is almost completely gone and forgotten but I'm like countless other people who don't need any lessons on 'real' life; we have seen and continue to see plenty of realism. I think art, in its various forms, should inspire as well as inform, should help as well as entertain people but I suppose if your view of life excludes hope and purpose, you might as well produce the kind of thing Samuel Beckett's thirty-five-second play, *Breath*, offers.

The props are a pile of rubbish on an empty stage, lit by a light which becomes a bit brighter and then dims away into darkness. There are no actors, no words, just a recorded cry, an inhaled breath, an exhaled breath which begins the play and an exhaled breath, an inhaled breath and a recorded cry at the close as the light goes out completely and leaves everything in darkness. That's Beckett's view of life. How's that for 'realism'? You can have it.

Film-makers and writers often brag about their 'realism', especially when they're giving the gory details on violence and filth. Life is grimy, they tell us. Of course, but should we brag about it? We should pin a medal on the producers of *Buddha in Suburbia* for parading our grimy lifestyle? Certainly it's raw but should we like it that way? Be proud of it? Should we help it to get grimier and grimier until underneath the filth we can't recognise the race and the standards by which we judge what is noble? Of course there's the Mafia and the porn kings and the people who have sex with toddlers, but should we shrug at it?

William Murchison said, 'It makes you want to peel a banana and scratch...'. We've gone 'in 30 years' from actors who act like people, to actors who, considering what they do on screen, would seem more at home in a nice zoological garden. It's true that literature and drama exemplify life but there are two ways to do it. One is to hold up the good (virtue, justice, courage, etc.) for admiration and imitation. The second is to hold up the cruel, crude and questionable and proudly refuse to contrast it *un*favourably with the good. Or to suggest that there is no difference between life-styles! You'd think at this time of crisis our artists would like to show us the alternatives—good people doing good things, as living commentary on the bad. No, the artists, the talk show hosts, wallow happily in the mud, oinking at those who dare to suggest man has a higher destiny than grabbing himself below the belt and blurting out cruelty and obscenities.

Anyway, I like films. Of all the films I've ever seen, two stand out as personal favourites: *Field of Dreams* runs a close but definite second to *The Miracle Worker*. *Miracle Worker* is about Annie Sullivan who gave a profound gift to the world—Helen Keller.

In Tuscumbia, Alabama in 1870 the Keller's baby girl fell ill and this resulted in her becoming blind, deaf and mute. She was nineteen-months-old. Without communication she grew into a 'little human animal', trapped in the silent darkness, a victim to moods and to the ways in which her sad parents spoiled her because they didn't know what else to do. 'Every day she slips further and further away,' said her mother, 'and I don't know how to call her back.'

Then Annie Sullivan arrived. She wasn't much more than a child herself, but she had known 'real' life and all the pain, frustration and heartache that goes with it. But her suffering had taught her toughness as well as compassion. She isn't long at the Keller's before Helen shows her that she knew the power of a key—she locks Sullivan in her room so she can't trouble her anymore. Annie, realising that she can't help Helen because the parents continue to interfere with her work with the girl, asks them to let her have complete control over the child, in a little summer house next to the main house. They take Helen for a long drive so she won't know where she is, they deposit her in the summer house and leave immediately.

By now Helen regards Sullivan as her tormentor so you can imagine her horror when she realises she is left alone with someone who will give her no peace. In panic she tries to find the door, to escape the clutches of this one who refuses to let her do as she wishes, but when she finds it, it's locked and the woman has the key. Locked in by sightless eyes and unhearing ears she's now locked in with her torturer.

For two weeks Sullivan 'torments' her, refusing to let her eat or sleep or play unless she is willing to abide by the rules. Tirelessly teaching her the letters of the alphabet on her hands and trying to get through to her that the 'words' stand for the 'things', that the 'things' have 'names' and that the shapes made by her fingers and hands are the letters which spell the names which stand for the things.

The two weeks fly by without a breakthrough, the parents can no longer stand the separation and resist Sullivan's pleas for more time. They take her back, prison's ended, torment's over, she's free again. As soon as she's back in the house, she goes around checking all the doors to see that they're unlocked and then she takes the key and puts it in her mother's pocket, making sure that her tormentor won't have power over her again. Then all the obedience and rules she has learned are tossed to the winds, back comes the animal behaviour which comes to a head when she throws a jug of water over the teacher. Sullivan ignores the protests of the parents, grabs the jug and Helen, drags her out to the pump, forces her to fill the jug with water while she spells W..A..T..E..R on the girl's fingers and hands.

And that's when it happens. All of a sudden Helen stops struggling, she throws away the jug and allows the water to run through her fingers as she strains to say the one word she had learned when she was a nineteen-month-old baby:

water! The light comes on in her mind, she struggles to work out what it means that WATER (what was being spelled out on her fingers) stands for what she feels pouring all over her hands. Her prison walls are collapsing, she now has a rational connection with her world, 'words' are 'things'. Afraid to believe in case she's mistaken she makes Sullivan pump more water, feels it, grabs her teacher's hand and spells out WATER? The teacher confirms it and slowly the tears begin to flow as freedom steals into her life. Ecstatically she wants to know the name of everything, the word for what's under her feet, for the soil she can pick up in her hands, for the thing the water comes out of. The father and mother join the celebration, there's crying and laughing as the girl communicates with the world around her and learns the name 'mother'.

She turns from her parents, finds Sullivan and asks her what her name is and Sullivan spells out 'teacher'. Softness and gratitude spread over her face. Slowly she finds her way back to her mother who holds her and doesn't want to let her go but she's groping for the key in her mother's pocket and wriggles free. Back she goes to the 'teacher', opens her hand and presses the key into it. Now she knows! Now she trusts! All along her tormentor had been her friend, the one who had been locking her in was wanting to set her free. What she needed all her life, unknown to her, was someone who would do less or more for her, she needed someone who would demand things of her, put her through some pain in order to right the wrong. *She learned there is more than one way to understand and respond to much of the pain of life.*

To say that God introduced evil and its consequences

into the world is a blunder but to insist that God brings good out of evil and richness out of suffering is something illustrated by the experience of Helen Keller. (Maybe we can all take another look at the grief-bringing situations in our lives.) An utterly brilliant movie because it dealt with an incredibly moving slice of life and because it has all kinds of messages for you and me. It beats Beckett's *Breath* or Kafka's *The Trial* to pieces.

THIRTEEN

I think I am to be envied

Everyone lives a life of self-denial. We all say 'no' to some things to get other things. We all say 'no' to things less important so we can say 'yes' to the more important. If someone wants to be a brilliant snooker-player, ice-skater, boxer, musician or other, they say goodbye to so much freedom. Swimmers have to spend endless hours in the pool, tennis players are on court until they're weary, musicians practise the scales until they play them in their sleep. People say 'no' to the extra slice of meat or bread to shed the unwanted pounds. It's thoughtlessness which makes us say we don't believe in sacrificing—we all do it, all of our lives.

Jesus lived a life of self-denial but so did Judas!

In Victor Hugo's, *Les Miserables,* the hero, Jean Valjean is established in life as Monsieur Madeleine, an upright citizen and acclaimed mayor of the town, Montreuil-sur-mer. He had been a criminal in the past but a compassion he couldn't fathom forced him to decide once and for all if he would live in hate and criminal bitterness or be the servant of God an old bishop had called him to be. For more than eight years he had served his people well and he fully intended to do more and to do it all his life.

But a police-inspector, Javert, who worships the law to

the point of idolatry, suspects that the mayor is none other than the former convict who robbed a little boy of some money and was never caught. The policeman works to prove his case but his superiors think him mad and threaten him with dismissal. Javert has taken note of Valjean's selflessness and pity on occasions and makes use of that insight when he comes to the mayor's office one day. He confesses to 'Madeleine' that he had suspected him of being the wanted criminal and for this detection he should be dismissed as inspector. He now knew he was wrong about the mayor, he said, since the real Valjean had been apprehended and was to be tried in a nearby town and (no doubt) imprisoned.

Valjean ponders what he should do. Expose his real identity and be imprisoned again? Bring to an end all the good he had been doing and would be able to do? Rake up a petty crime which happened years earlier and bring crashing down all the wonderful plans for the well-being of perhaps thousands of people? And, then, there were those who had become precious to him at a personal level; what of them? No, he couldn't desert them! And besides, he couldn't face that prison again!

But he cannot rest and goes to the town and to the court and there sees familiar faces—his former prison mates. He hears the mistaken testimony, identifying the man as Valjean and the one guilty of robbing the boy. Sentence is about to be pronounced when the pain-filled mayor makes himself known, establishes his identity and accepts the court's judgement. Released, on the understanding that he would shortly deliver himself up for punishment, Valjean leaves the courtroom which is filled with sympathetic and astonished people. About to go out of the door, he stops and says to the packed room which recognises the nobility and gallantry of the man, 'You who are here present, find me deserving of pity, do you not? For myself, when I consider what I came so near to doing, I think I am to be envied…'

Don't you love that? This is only possible to a person of clear and grand vision. It isn't just a matter of intellect; it's a question of moral vision. It's a question of values. It's a way of looking at things. Ethics, before it is a way of *doing* things is a way of *seeing* things. In this case, Valjean saw honour and justice as of more value than his freedom. He consigned himself to prison again and was glad to do it when he considered that he was about to allow an innocent man to suffer for his crime.

To give the gift of honourable vision is a precious gift indeed. A lot of people slide noiselessly into the darkness, in part, because they haven't seen the glory of nobility or been inspired by grander models. It isn't enough to make demands of people for higher living; it's important for us to motivate each other to these higher levels. And it's a blunder of terrible proportions to give the impression that it is only kind, compassionate and faithful people who practise self-denial. Where they follow the higher vision they are simply saying 'no' to the base to gain the precious. In the end, it's those who reject faithfulness and fairness and sacrificial living who really 'deny themselves' and cheapen all that they are and were intended by God to be. The parable of 'pearl of great price' (Matthew 13) has much to teach all of us.

FOURTEEN

Things I always meant to do

Do I need to tell any of you how distressed I am at times over lost opportunities to do good, express love, speak a word for Christ? Haven't you experienced the same thing? My intentions to be kind and caring to people, tomorrow, goes on the assumption that those I wish to reach will be around tomorrow!

Once when my mother wasn't feeling very well I went by to see her. The house was tiny, the stairs to the little bedroom were steep and her bed, while not large, seemed huge as she lay there (she wasn't five feet tall). We talked a while and as I was leaving, I stood behind the bedroom door and worked up the nerve to tell her I loved her. (Don't ask me why it was difficult—I don't know. I have always blamed it on one thing or another.) She didn't respond and I glanced around the door and she was quietly weeping. If I'd only known. The last time I saw my little mother she was crying at our door as my family and I were leaving the country for a while. I told her it wouldn't be long until I was back but she died before I had the chance to fulfil my intentions—to 'really' show her what love is. No, it isn't true. I *did* see her one more time—— when I came back for the funeral—I whispered to her and kissed her. I blundered terribly. Friends have moved away and I've lost track of them. How I wish, I tell myself, I had been more of a friend when the opportunity was there. I am determined to do what I know I should do (as much as I am able) and to do the things I'm stirred to do, promptly! Some sad and remorseful girl wrote this poem which has haunted me since I read it in a Buscaglia book. It's called:

Things You Didn't Do.

Remember the day I borrowed your brand new car and I
*   dented it?*
I thought you'd kill me; but you didn't.
And remember the day I dragged you to the beach, and
*   you said it would rain, and it did?*
I thought you'd say: I told you so! And you didn't.
Do you remember the time I flirted with all the guys to
*   make you jealous and you were?*
I thought you'd leave me; but you didn't.
Do you remember the time I spilt strawberry pie all over
*   your car rug?*
I thought you'd hit me, but you didn't.
And remember the time I forgot to tell you the dance was
*   formal and you showed up in jeans?*
I thought you'd drop me, but you didn't.
Yes, there were lots of things you didn't do.
But you put up with me, and you loved me and
*   protected me.*
There were lots of things I wanted to make up to you
*   when you returned from Viet Nam.*
But you didn't.

I want to love and serve and cherish and confront and comfort and inspire **now**! I don't want to develop the habit of putting off the good I know and feel like doing. And I will not let my failures to fulfil this purpose overwhelm me. I've made up my mind and by the grace of God I'll see it through. I know I won't be perfect in anything. But I will improve! I will exercise myself unto service, moment by moment, opportunity by opportunity. I will not wait until the 'significant' occasion arises. I know if I am faithful a little that the 'much' will take care of itself under God's hand. From this moment on I will have fewer bitter memories of things I didn't do and more joy in the realisation that I've been a channel of blessing to some people a little but in significant ways by 'doing it now'.

SECTION FOUR:
THOSE WHO'LL STAY

ONE

The struggler's need of those who'll stay

The ancient British warriors must have looked long and hard when they first saw the Roman troops land on their beaches. They would have seen them form ranks and stand to attention while their boats were burned before their eyes. Whatever else these Romans had in mind, they weren't planning to go home —soon—they had come to stay.

And some centuries earlier, when Xerxes with his vast army made a move on Greece they came to a narrow mountain pass called Thermopylae. The report from the scouts said there was a handful of desperate Greeks who were going to dispute the pass with him and what was more, many of these Greeks (Spartans) were performing gymnastics and brushing their long hair. The 'Great King' couldn't believe it. He conferred with Damaratus, an exiled Spartan king, and was told that this was a Spartan death ritual. These men were specially chosen. Most of them were without wives and children and they were not planning on going home—they had come to stay. Xerxes offered them their lives if they would simply surrender but they turned it down and paid with their lives. Their example set Greece alight and Xerxes lost the next two battles before sailing home.

It's this 'I've come to stay' spirit which is so impressive. Aren't there too many promises made which aren't kept? Too many covenants made which are broken when times get tough? On the other side there are millions of people whose predictability is a wonder to behold. They came and stayed.

It's people who change people and it's love that binds. There are those who so live their lives that even after they're gone they are still with us like a fragrance that hangs over our lives. They came and stayed in life and because they stayed in life they remain after death.

But there's no drama in most of it as there is in the story of the 300 Spartans. Lives are lived in quietness, no trumpets blowing or red carpets. Days becomes weeks, months and years without fuss; but there's devotion, courage, gentleness, sacrifice and cheerfulness. Friends stand by friends at awful cost or inspire each other with unfailing (but judicious) praise and shining example. Families bear unutterable pain together and dismiss it all with self-effacing remarks. Marriages do more than survive tremendous pressures as a couple keep their promise to each other:

I'll never leave you. Others may come and go in your life. I never will. If you're sick I'll nurse you, feed you, bathe you, sit up with you. Anything but leave you. I'll never leave you.

(Saunders)

TWO

Middle 'C'

I like my wife Ethel for a lot of reasons and her predictability is one of them. I can be sure of Ethel. When I used to travel quite a bit she would pack my bags for me and never forget anything and she would invariably stick a love note in a sock or a shirt pocket. When I got back, there she was at the airport to drive me home. When I had finished my early evening jog and was soaking my poor body in the tub she'd always be singing in the kitchen directly below me as she got our evening meal ready. Lovely! All these bits and pieces were only expressions of what was there as bedrock—she was never going to leave, she was always wanting the best for me and always doing what she thought helped me to do my best. Those who've never experienced that kind of lovely predictability (or who can't remember having experienced it) have lived a genuinely deprived life.

I have a lovely niece, Pat, who lives in Australia. A few years ago when I was in Sydney on business I visited the family in Melbourne and discovered my sister was very ill with cancer. Kathleen (Pat's mother) made her peace with God and life and then some months later she died. Pat had been struggling for some time to find her way in what had been a life with some major difficulties.

She and Kathleen would get together for some 'straight

talking on a regular basis. A week or so after Kathleen went away Pat wrote me and told me she missed her mother for numerous reasons but one of them has stuck with me. She said no matter how far she moved she could always look around to see that Kathleen was still there because Pat knew her mother was stability, a landmark, if you like, so that the daughter could always stay in contact with reality. It's great to have someone to whom you can look to check your bearings.

So much changes, so many voices call, so many passions rule, so many pressures blind or deafen us or *bewilder* us. We need some certainties, some 'sure things' by which to steer through life. Every boy or girl or man or woman who is that to someone else is doing a service beyond measure.

Colin Morris says that when Lloyd C. Douglas was a university student he had digs in a big house, on the ground floor of which lived an old music teacher, house-bound due to some illness. Douglas would visit him every day, popping his head around the door and asking the same ritual question, 'Well, what's the good news today?' And he would get the same ritual answer. The old man would pick up a tuning fork and strike it on the table. 'Hear that? It's Middle "C". It is Middle "C" today. It was Middle "C" yesterday and the day before. It will be Middle "C" tomorrow and the day after and for a thousand years to come. The tenor across the hall sings flat and the piano upstairs is out of tune. Noise! Noise all around me, but that, my friend is Middle "C".'

I love that story. In a world that's 'out of tune' in so many ways, where disharmony and flatness make us wince, it's great to know that some things are constant and that harmony is possible. *Hummmmmm.*

A Bible writer had this grand word to say which should comfort the whole wide world. 'Never will I leave you; never will I forsake you.' And a few sentences later he says, 'Jesus Christ is the same yesterday and today and forever.' These truths, which are so hard for some of us to believe, are made concrete for us in so many lovely experiences and people in life. The joy of returning to a warm and welcoming home, the blessed relief when you've finally shouldered the responsibility for your wrong, the pleasure you find in a genuine friendship, the power you feel when you have one noble, driving purpose or the humble feeling you have when you see innocent trust in a child. By these solid, glorious realities God would help us to rise to him who, in his intentions toward humanity, is changeless. Part of the good news, says A. J. Gossip, 'is that once you've met God in Christ, really met Him and know you've met Him, you know Him forever because He never changes.'

When the sight of a cemetery, overgrown with weeds, assaults our minds; when the cell door clangs shut and the lights go out, when the economy falters just long enough for our business to collapse or when a rocky marriage is finally tossed aside by one who doesn't care to make it work, when the child has been diagnosed as having cystic fibrosis or they're cutting off your electricity because you can't pay the bill—when things like these happen there is noise! Clamour! Disharmony! Look around for a friend and, hard as it may be for you, listen for the *hummmmmm*. You might do what I've done, if you can afford it, buy a tuning-fork and carry it around with you. *Hummmmmm.*

THREE

'Free-Love'?

G. K. Chesterton led an interesting and fruitful life. He said of himself, 'I was a pagan at the age of twelve, and a complete agnostic by the age of sixteen.' He said he never read any Christian material but that his reading of Herbert Spencer's agnostic lectures gave him his first 'wild doubts about doubt' and his reading of the atheist, Ingersoll, made him think, 'almost thou persuadest me to be a Christian.' He had a common sense way about him and his writings brought truth to his readers in a wonderful readable way. Here's the kind of thing I mean. He's talking about people who attack the making of binding commitments, vows, and especially the marriage covenant. They were saying that such vows hindered love; that love mustn't be bound by such things as marriage: 'It is most amusing to listen to opponents of marriage on this subject. They appear to imagine that the ideal of constancy was a yoke mysteriously imposed by the devil, instead of being, as it is, a yoke imposed by lovers on themselves. They have invented a phrase that is a black-and-white contradiction in two words—'free-love'—as if a lover ever had been, or ever could be, free. It is of the nature of love to bind itself, and the institution of marriage merely paid the average man the compliment of taking him at his word.' Yes!

What drove tiny May Lempke to adopt Leslie, an abandoned blind infant with cerebral palsy; to nurse, bathe, massage, feed, carry, talk to and pray for for nearly sixteen years before she heard a single word from him? Nurturing and blessing him until one day he sat down at a piano and, amazingly, began to play classical music to perfection. Bless her, she couldn't do anything else, she loved the child!

For love of the poor children, Thomas John Barnardo founded more than ninety homes for the destitute and earned himself the name 'Father of Nobody's Children'.

Lord Shaftesbury, who spent a huge fortune as one loving-expression of his care for poor children, had died. On hearing the news, one poorly-dressed boy anxiously asks the other, 'That's not *our* Lord Shaftesbury, is it?' The second one says, 'Yes, it's *our* Lord Shaftesbury.'

Having suffered so much when she and her little brother were inexcusably shoved into a lunatic asylum (where the little boy died), we would have excused young Annie Sullivan if, complaining about her own failing sight, she had lived a life of whimpering selfishness, but she didn't. For love of people and love of learning she threw herself into the rescue of Helen Keller who has blessed the world in so many ways. Annie, like all the world's great lovers wasn't free to choose because 'it is of the nature of love to bind itself.' Friends don't want to be free. Parents don't want to be free. Lovers don't want to be free. We've all known the joy of giving rather than taking. We've not sunk so far that we've never known a time when we denied ourselves something so that one we loved was provided for. We see it in crowded hospital waiting-rooms where families sit, sometimes day and night for long periods, even when they've been told there is nothing they can do. 'Oh, but he might wake up and I'd want to be here!' 'She'd worry if I wasn't around.' Nobody forces lovers into some kind of bondage, they joyfully choose the 'burden' that love brings with it.

In a house on the Shankill Road in Belfast I sat, saddened and almost speechless, looking at twelve-year-old Jim who had just lost his grandad, as eight-year-old Aaron, tear-filled and silent, sat on the arm of the chair with his arm around his best friend's shoulders. That image, which will stay in my mind all my life, said again that there is no 'free' love! We pay a painful price for the privilege of being lovers. We see it at airports, bus-stations, train-stations and at harbours. Hearts breaking because someone more precious to us than ourselves is going away and while they must go we don't want them to leave. And we know exactly how the poet felt when he wrote this of his beloved:

> I will not let thee go
> The stars that crowd the summer skies
> Have watched us here below
> With all their million eyes,
> I dare not let thee go...
> I hold thee by too many bands:
> Thou sayest farewell, and lo!
> I have thee by the hands,
> And will not let thee go.

It has nothing to do with rules or regulations, has it? The famous Saul of Tarsus runs off across the world to spread the message about the one he calls his Lord. He claims he has no choice but to speak as he does but when you ask him what it is that compels him to suffer so much and speak as he does, he just says, 'The love of Christ.' There is no 'free' love! So it isn't really surprising to read in the Bible, 'God so loved that he gave...'

FOUR

Of mothers and grandmothers

How many sights do you know that are more lovelier than a fully grown man tenderly taking his elderly mother's arm and helping her as she walks from the car to the front door or from the waiting room to the doctor? What do you know that's warmer than glancing in to see a grandmother reading a story to a child who sits transfixed or lies in peace or giggles like mad on her lap? Young mothers are beautiful but what is it about a white-haired, elderly mother who stills tenderly touches her fifty-year-old son and flattens his hair down as she did all those years ago when he couldn't do it for himself?

B. G. White of Jacksonville, Florida wasn't eavesdropping but was glad she heard what she heard. It was mid-October, and the trees along the Blue Ridge Parkway were ablaze with colour. At a place where all this could be appreciated she stood next to a woman who was showing the view to her elderly mother. 'Isn't it wonderful of God to take something just before it dies and make it so beautiful?' the daughter said as she looked at some of the fallen leaves. 'Wouldn't it be nice,' the mother mused, 'if he did that with people?' The younger woman looked at the white-haired stooped figure beside her and said so softly that she thought no one else heard, 'Sometimes he does.'

I know that civilised societies and countries are held together by governments which seek the welfare of the law-abiding majority. I know that and I'm grateful for it. I know that society is blessed by devoted schoolteachers, social workers, just judges and idealistic lawyers. I've seen what passionate men and women can do for societies when they embody noble principles at the centres of power. And only a fool can dismiss as nothing the thousands of community organisations in the cities and towns of the world which cater to the emotional and physical needs of countless unfortunate people. But all these beautiful men and women had mothers and grandmothers (or those who stood in the place of mothers and grandmothers) who helped to shape their characters. For good or evil it's people who change people and there are no people who change people more than mothers and grandmothers!

One little boy put it very well when asked what a grandmother was. He said, 'A grandmother is a lady who has no children of her own so she loves everybody else's. Grandmas don't have anything to do except be there. If they take you for a walk they slow down past leaves and caterpillars. They never say "hurry up". Usually they're fat, but not too fat to tie your shoes. They wear glasses and sometimes they can take their teeth out. They can answer questions like why dogs hate cats and why God isn't married. When they read to you they don't skip words or mind if it's the same story again. Everyone should try to have a grandmother, especially if they don't have television because grandmas are the only grown-ups who always have time for you.'

Mothers and grandmothers have been praised since the world began. One of the most famous men in history was writing encouragement to a young man he knew, urging him to gallantly complete a difficult commission he had been given. In the course of it he reminded the young man of the splendour of the lives of his grandmother (Lois) and mother (Eunice) and in this way he urged him to live nobly.

The famous man was Paul, a special messenger of Jesus Christ, and his young friend was Timothy. And did the young man follow in the steps of his mother and grand-mother, living his life nobly? Tradition says he became a leading figure for many years in the Christian movement in Ephesus and that he was clubbed to death by a maddened mob because he publicly denounced the frenzy and immo-rality of worship to the Ephesian goddess, Artemis (Diana).

A grandmother and her daughter took a little boy of nervous temperament and helped shape him into a kind but bold spokesman for societal righteousness and decency. It shouldn't be hard for us to see Timothy spend time giggling and thoughtful, wide-eyed and sleepy, quiet and question-ing in the laps of the two most important and influential people in his life as he was being moulded to play his part in the changing of the world for the better.

B. G. White's young woman was right, sometimes God takes something before it dies and makes it so beautiful— white-haired, stooped little mothers and grandmothers for example.

FIVE

You promised

'I stretch myself into unpredictable days ahead and make one thing predictable for you—I will be there with you.' That's how Lewis Smedes opens a book of his. He goes on to say, 'We have a mystery on our hands…it is the mystery of how we, weak and limited persons that we are, can look at all the uncertainty of life full in the face and say, I will make one thing certain: my presence in the life of another.'

As someone who knows plenty about failure to keep promises I've got to say that that kind of talk makes me want to be trustworthy in every area of my life and to a greater degree than have been. I'm convinced by it (of course!) but at one and the same time I'm inspired and made wistful by it. I haven't been a total failure (have any of us?) but I've known more than my share of disappointing God and people when it came to being where I said I'd be.

It's possible of course that I'm enamoured by *the words* and the potential in them for a touching, memorable sermon or article. On the other hand—and God alone can tell—maybe there's within me and everybody else who feels a deep sense of failure, an unsatisfied longing for the wealth of inspiration and challenge the words bring. Words, used by God to take the limp sails of a half-decent, fairly motivated life and fill them with the wind of God. Fill them to their capacity, great or small, so that they drive us on through the seas of life with power and purpose. To keep our promises, to carve out, by God's grace, one piece of the uncertain future and make it certain for someone.

It could hardly be surprising to hear me say that only God does this flawlessly. The book of *Exodus* reminds us that God is trustworthy, that He keeps his promises. Exodus 2:24; 3:6,8, 13–17; 4:5 and 6:2–8 reminds us that what happened in those days was the inevitable result of God being the kind of God who keeps His word, who lives the love He promises. He acted for Israel (and the world) against Egypt because He promised Abraham something. In the midst of centuries filled with the unpredictable, there was always God's promise they could bank on. Romans 8:31–39 insists that God will allow us to face unpredictable futures but that those uncertainties in no way will affect the certainty of His loving presence.

And while it's true that God knows better than we, that we're sinful and weak, that we get weary with the unending task (yes, task as well as privilege) He doesn't exempt us from the call to keep our covenants. There is no life with God outside a covenantal relationship and with one another. We who would find a covenant too great a commitment to make or too much trouble to try to live in, will find ourselves without life with God.

So whether we're wives/husbands, friends, children/parents, brothers/sisters, fellow-disciples or fellow-humans—we're called to keep our promises. If we are not willing to make the effort (and that's for God and us to know), we are not willing to have life with Him.

All the previous, I suppose, is obvious and straight forward. What follows is complex, in need of balancing and correction, depending on varying circumstances. Sinners like us are afflicted with all the symptoms of sin.

Some of us are tempted terribly quickly to 'forgive ourselves'. Years ago Robert Mackintosh gave us this chilling but not unnecessary word about repentance, 'Those who are in a hurry to forgive themselves, and who find the valley of humiliation unendurable, have reason to fear that they are hurrying away from God.' Others are sorely tempted to self-righteousness and I seem to recall Jesus addressing that on more than one occasion.

Some of us live with the unceasing pain of failures we can't forgive ourselves for—as though forgiveness was our prerogative. And some of us are cruelly tempted to act as judge on a sinner's desires and efforts. That's an area in which we are utterly incompetent. I mention these four faces of sin to help keep us, maybe, from making hard and fast judgements too quickly.

If we are not willing to have an honest shot at living up to the noble and gallant promises of 'being there' let's not pretend we are. Few things are as discouraging as sweet words, fine articles, great sermons and consistently savage behavior. We can create a world of cynics by an endless stream of the right sounds spoken in a confident tone and accompanied with contrary behaviour. So at least let's tone down the language we use until we're prepared to pay the price of an honest-to-goodness pursuit of our promises.

On the other hand, if we are not willing to make some deep covenantal promises that we're not prepared to 'live up to' we need to ask ourselves again if we want life with God. To make loving commitments in one area or another is essential since there is no life outside a covenantal status. It means we freely choose to limit our freedom. Let me share again these words from Chesterton. He said critics of marriage covenants 'appear to imagine that the ideal of constancy was a yoke mysteriously imposed by the devil, instead of being, as it is, a yoke imposed by lovers on themselves. They invented a phrase that is a black-and-white contradiction in two words—'free love'—as if a lover ever had been, or ever could be, free. It is of the nature of love to bind itself, and the institution of marriage merely paid the average man the compliment of taking him at his word.' Yes! Whether its friendship, marriage, brother or sisterhood—lovers don't wish to be free. At least let's quit kidding ourselves. If we make loving promises we need to recognise that it's going to cost us. When the time comes to pay the price we mustn't protest that we didn't know what we were getting into. (Balance all of this where it needs balancing.)

All of this should help us to temper our language, should help to keep us from using speech too lavish or glibly making promises we really don't mean to keep. Perhaps Smedes' call will help us to count the cost and make the commitment with eyes wide open and hearts full of noble purpose so that when we're tempted to ease back, those to whom we made our commitment can call us back to the task with two words: *You promised!*

SIX

In praise of the quiet ones

The author, George Eliot, spoke the truth when she said that things in life were not so hard with many of us as they might have been because of people who now lie in unvisited graves. The silent ones, the unheralded people, those who go through life helpful, dependable, solid, but without fanfare or commotion. They're the kind who take a lot of photographs but are rarely in them. They are mothers and fathers, they are older sisters and brothers who have taken on responsibilities when the parents were too old or tired to see to them. They came into our lives to stay and remain even when they have gone.

The columnist, Erma Bombeck, had a father just like that. She said her father was like a refrigerator light. Every house had one but nobody knew what either of them did when the door was shut. But he was there when her roller-skates needed oiling or when it was raining hard and somebody had to bring the car round to the door; he was there to fix clothe-lines or steady a person when they were learning to ride a bike. He was the only one in the house who wasn't afraid to go places in the dark, he left for work early in the morning and always seemed glad to see everyone at night. One day he didn't get up and go to work, he went to hospital and died the next day. And out of her life but not out of her heart went one of the quiet ones. They never do anything special or flamboyant so why is there such an ache when they leave? An ache that has its hideout but is never far away.

That's how my eldest brother, Willie, was. A deep-voiced, solid man who worked every day in a Belfast firm called Wilson Engineering. He had been a 'shot-blaster' (we used to call it 'sand-blaster') which meant he cleaned up the cast iron objects when they came out of the furnace and had cooled down. It was heavy work, and dirty, as are most of the jobs in a foundry and Willie's health wasn't great. He had to quit that job so they moved him on to something not as physically demanding but he had a coronary blockage and died at the age of fifty. (Dear God, was he that young?)

There was a quietness about him, a deliberateness. He worked not a half mile from our house and I can still see him (after these many years), hands in his pockets, covered in grime, whistling as he walked with the peculiar 'McGuiggan walk', coming in his lunch-hour to see how our mother was getting on.

Willie was good at fixing things; chairs, cupboards, book-shelves, simple mechanical things and he'd usually whistle while he was getting on with it.

My nephew, Alex, recently told me that his mother, Elizabeth ('Lizzie') was the more vocal of the two but when his father died he observed she was noticeably quieter. It seemed to him that Willie was the quiet strength behind her ability to be decisive and self-assured and when he died she couldn't carry that role alone. Lizzie and Willie raised five wonderful children who are having their own quiet effect on this world.

Doing wonderful things behind the scenes is possible for even prominent people. There are those who, though they are prominent in the community, do so much good without fanfare because they are able to 'live without applause'. An accountant friend of mine was driving me from the airport in Dallas, Texas when we began to discuss two mutual friends. He was telling me he came across cheques written by these two men on behalf of so many worthy causes that it took his breath away.

A.C. Benson told of a visit to an old doctor by a man who suffered greatly as a result of overwork and depression. After a careful examination, the old man talked with him, advising, relieving his mind and in the process, helping him greatly. The patient wrote in his dairy about that visit: 'I looked at the worn face and kind eyes of the man whose life is spent in plumbing the depths of human suffering. What a terrible life, and yet what a noble one! He spoke as though he had no other case in the world to consider except my own; yet, when I went back to the waiting-room to get my hat, and looked around at the anxious-looking crowd of patients waiting there, each with a secret burden, I felt how heavy a load he must be carrying.' The doctor's name isn't given. Another of the awesome 'quiet ones'.

SEVEN

Maria

If only we would tone down our extravagant speech and leave it to the poets or keep our promises, we would produce fewer cynics. It just isn't good enough to make the commitment and then, when we see it's going to cost a bit more than we envisaged, to behave as though our word means nothing. This is not only a personal failure, it helps to create a climate, even a culture.

A recent TV commercial. A radiant, beautifully dressed woman, runs down the steps of a grand building. She makes her way through a crowd of deliriously happy people who are shouting best wishes to her. 'All the best in your new life' or 'have a wonderful life.' They're throwing confetti, laughing and patting her. She climbs into a beautiful car, it pulls away, it has boots and tins tied to the back. She is thrilled to pieces, takes off her ring and throws it out of the window and as the car pulls away we see the attached sign: *Just Divorced*. What do you think? A mark of our culture?

And it isn't as though people can't keep their promises. I confess I grow weary with the claim that young people can't keep covenants. They're doing it in their millions in every generation. And we hear that people can't keep marriage covenants while millions are doing it right before our eyes on every street in every city throughout the world. Yes, there are those of us who will not stay when we said we would; but that's just it, we *will* not stay. Aside from exceptional circumstances, we could if we would! Some of us use people and then toss them aside like paper plates or used 'Q Tips'.

We hear horror stories like that all the time. I read of one man who was wrongfully imprisoned; who insisted that while he had a criminal record he was not guilty of the crime for which he was jailed. If only he had the money to get a good lawyer he would be let out. His wife went to work, took in washing and cleaned offices at night for several years to get the money for the lawyer. The money was saved, the lawyer was hired and the man freed from prison. He left his wife a month later for a young girl who took his fancy. Don't tell me he *had* to leave her! He could have been manly and grateful and faithful had he *wanted* to.

We need people who come to stay! Michael Green wrote *Jesus Spells Freedom*. There he tells us of a seventeen-year-old girl called Maria Sorensino. In the 1940s Ezio Barberi and his ruthless gang achieved fame as a result of brutal murders and armed robberies. In 1949 he was sentenced to fifty-seven years in the maximum security wing of San Vitorre prison in Milan. He was a thug outside and he was a thug inside. He was involved in violence and rioting in the jail and, as is often the case, he had his cell walls covered in porn.

What has all this to do with Maria? Well, for some reason Maria had fixed her eye on Barberi and kept a

159

scrapbook of the gangster's moves and escapades. She took him into her heart and prayed for him every day. They had never met but she began writing to him in prison— regularly. She pleaded with him for change, expressed her love for him and despite his violent and ugly spirit she made a commitment to him and wouldn't turn from it.

Gradually Barberi began to change. Being on the receiving end of a love like that, said Green, began to transform him. He began to write to her, he ripped the porn off his wall and put her picture up, he responded to her tender letters with tenderness such as he had never shown to anyone. His violent behaviour ceased and Ezio became a model prisoner. He involved himself in the work of the hospital, charity endeavours and socially useful works. What happened to the cold-blooded, hate-filled criminal? Someone had come to stay. Someone paid the price for years without complaint and on 18 June 1968, twenty-one years (believe I'll say that again, twenty-one years) after Maria had entered his life, they were married in the prison chapel.

Yes, I know about the 'failures' of loving commitment (though nothing ever lovingly and honourably given is ever wasted), but people like Maria Sorensino are a sight for sore eyes in a world where cruelty, ingratitude and self-serving get centre stage. They are a rebuke to all this bleating and whinging about how hard it is to hang-in when things are tough or not moving as quickly in the right direction as we would wish.

I have no criticism whatever for those who for years have endured pain so stark that to be glib about it would be

obscene. I have no criticism for those who having endured
this state of affairs decided to call the relationship to a halt.
How could I whose life has been so easy?

And I'm wondering as I write this if there is *anyone*, alive
or dead, who could say of us that we came to stay and
stayed? And ringing in my head are the words of One who
said, 'I will never leave you, nor will I ever forsake you.'

EIGHT

'But I have forgtten his name'

'It was a bitterly cold night but these two old women had braved the cold wind and made their way to the place where I was speaking. When it was all over I was standing close to the door and just had to tell these two how nice it was of them to make the effort. I took the hand of the older lady in both my hands and with genuine warmth told her it was lovely to see her on such a terrible night. 'What's your name?' I asked, and for several seconds she couldn't remember. Her good friend began to laugh at her and, smiling, I quickly asked her what her name was. She couldn't remember hers either! Isn't that amazing? Mark you, neither of them was senile; far from it. For some reason, they just couldn't come up with their own names.

In another place and at another time I was passing a small group of women who were oohing and aahing at a new baby which the young mother was showing off (quite right too) to the surrounding admirers. I glanced in but they shut me out, so as I walked off one of the women asked the baby's name. There was silence and the young mother looked like she'd just been shot. She couldn't remember the baby's name. Isn't that amazing?

Ralph Waldo Emerson, the famous American writer, was a month short of eighty when he died. Both his body and mind were feeble in his later years and his memory loss was especially marked. A prominent (and respectable) collector of famous autographs had been granted permission to secure Emerson's. He arrived on schedule, was shown into the study where, seated in a huge chair behind a large desk was the famous man himself, old, tired and vague. The gentleman made the request that Emerson write him his autograph. Autograph? Yes, his name. Name? Yes, *his* name. Emerson had the gentleman write for him, Ralph Waldo Emerson, after which the once brilliant man, copied, with numerous glances to make sure he was doing it correctly, what his visitor had written. That isn't amazing and it makes me sad.

Emerson and Henry Wadsworth Longfellow, another American literary giant, had been friends for years. They shared not only a love of but a reputation in literature, they were about the same age, they married and lost their first wives at about the same time, both remarried around the same time and both came through some serious spiritual struggles. Emerson, who was to die a month later, attended the funeral of his friend despite his own feebleness and diminished mental capacity. He looked at the coffin and said, 'The gentleman who lies here was a beautiful soul, but I have forgotten his name.' That's sad but it's also incredibly lovely.

Hugh Black rightly said that it's a happy man who has so lived that when all else is forgotten, even his name, the memory of his life can never die. Such an effect had Longfellow's life on Emerson that while his powers were so far gone that he couldn't remember his friend's name, he couldn't forget his friend's life.

What George Eliot, the famous English author, wrote in her book, *Middlemarch*, produces in me the same warm feeling I get when I think of Emerson and Longfellow. 'The growing good of the world is partly dependent on unhistoric acts; and that things are not so ill with you and me as they might have been, is half owing to the number who have lived faithfully a hidden life, and rest in unvisited tombs.' There are those who came, and contrary to appearances they have stayed.

Bill Smith's father was dying. He was so far gone that there was no reaction whatever when the much-loved, immediate family told him who they were and spoke their love to him right at the end. But when Bill whispered the name of Jesus in his ear, from some vast depths of his being the older man found the power to make a visible response. When all other names, even those of his adoring family, were powerless, that name moved him.

In his *A Death in the Desert*, Robert Browning tells of the approaching death of John the only remaining apostle of Jesus Christ. Those with him were hungry to hear more from the dying man but all attempts to ward off the approach of death proved fruitless until the boy with them was 'stung by the splendour of a sudden thought' ran off and came back with a plate with scripture engraved on it and began to read, 'I am the resurrection and the life...' The words of Jesus moved the old man who opened his eyes wide, sat up and began to speak.

Uniquely, Jesus came and contrary to appearances, He has stayed. Though all names may be forgotten this name will one day be acknowledged by the whole human race.

NINE

Didn't our hearts burns

Over and over again I hear people say that values and good behaviour can't be taught. People like Hiram Ginott and Albert Schweitzer claimed that such things can only be taught by example but I read that in their *books* so they must be overstating their case. So while I hold that values and other things like that can be taught verbally, I can't help thinking that such people should be pardoned their exaggeration. For good or evil, it's people who change people by their life-style and attitudes—as well as by their books and lectures.

Self help material calls at us from every book shop, information is poured into us from lecterns and pulpits. If people were changed by mere verbalising, we'd be living in a virtual paradise or a virtual hell, depending on who is speaking and what is being said. But it takes more than 'knowing' what to do in order to change or endure or be inspired. We need to be 'fired-up'. To be grabbed, seized and carried along by some glorious passion if we are to be delivered from apathy, vile habits or the tendency to fold under pressure. And there are few things, if any, more exciting as being a friend to someone who, by his/her life, sets your life on fire.

Somewhere it's written that two men met a man and after he left them, they said to each other, 'Didn't our hearts burn within us as he walked with us on the road?'

A lot of information given to us to help us be enriched is very good as far as it goes; but it's good for the already receptive people. It has more of the nature of fuel than fire. Much of the teaching is 'more food' laid out before people with no appetite. It is good, dry, easy to ignite fuel, piled up in a fireless grate. What it lacks is a spark, what the hearers lack is hunger.

If you were to ask a large number of people who feel they've really changed for the better and to what they credit the change, you'd find they point to people, friends, family or a teacher.

Sir Thomas Foxwell Burton found just such a family in the Earlhams. This is what he said, 'I know of no blessing of a temporal nature for which I ought to render so many thanks as my connection with the Earlham family; it has given colour to my whole life. They were eager for improvement; I caught the infection. At the college of Dublin, at a distance from all my friends and all control, their influence and the desire to please them kept me hard at my books and sweetened the toil they gave. The distinctions I gained at college were exclusively the result of the animating passion in my mind to carry back to them the prizes which they had prompted and enabled me to win.' *People* change people.

And it isn't necessary that there be many people in order for change to be effected. We need only a few (maybe one) and if they're passionate enough, they can set a whole movement or a society on fire.

Years ago Arnold Bennett divided society into two classes—the 'crowd' and the 'passionate few' and from there went on to show the power of the 'passionate few'. It isn't the masses that keep the name of Shakespeare vibrant and alive—it's the 'passionate few'. It's the 'passionate few' Wordsworthians or Tennysonians who keep the names of Wordsworth and Tennyson alive and to be reckoned with. It's the same in the religious realm. The bulk of us are and have been kept in touch with the magic of Jesus Christ as a result of the 'passionate few'. We bump against them and felt the heat, began to wonder and then were smitten by their passion). They embodied glorious truths, they had a 'fever' for Christ and we caught the infection and were dazzled by the glory.

SECTION FIVE:
FORGIVENESS

ONE

The struggler's need of forgiveness

To say something very profound about the rich notion of 'forgiveness' is not only beyond the scope of this little book, it is beyond my competence; but it won't hurt to say some things in passing.

It's only in speech or writing that forgiveness is thought to be easy or cheap. When it comes to practising it, we can find a hundred reasons (good reasons, of course!) why we shouldn't forgive. Far removed from actual offences, painful and often-repeated offences, we can talk glibly about forgiving. When we have been gouged, or worse, when some much-loved friend or family member has been gouged—when that happens, the words about forgiveness are sometimes dismissed or qualified beyond recognition. This may be perfectly understandable but it underscores the reality we wrestle with in this area.

Still, we mustn't expect badly wounded people to dispense forgiveness the way a cigarette machine dispenses cigarettes. There aren't many things harder to swallow than to watch serious offenders further hurt the ones they've wounded with a (virtual) demand for forgiveness even while the wounded are anguished with the pain. We

171

can't *demand* what can only be a gift of grace! As World War II ended, numerous guards and camp commandants sought forgiveness from those they treated so horrendously and were refused it. Is that really surprising? I'm not saying forgiveness should have been withheld; I just want to make the point that a lot of glib rot is spoken about forgiveness by those who've never suffered at any deeper level at the hands of transgressors.

I'm saying that forgiveness doesn't come easy to people who've been terribly used and abused by offenders. Even the saintly Corrie Ten Boom confessed, at one point, to having a very difficult time indeed in forgiving her Nazi enemies. When we see remarkable cases of forgiveness in the face of awful sin we're amazed and inspired by it. If it were common to see fearful transgressions graciously forgiven we'd cease to be amazed.

My limited observation on life suggests it's often the case that the very upright and law-abiding people, or those who see themselves in this light, have an especially tough time forgiving. They often lack patience and tolerance with offenders. The fact that their own lives are under control, that their behaviour and speech are impeccable leads them to believe that everyone's life should be like that. If they can control themselves, it must be that everyone can—if indeed they wish to. If they are not controlled, why then, they must wish not to be controlled and if they don't wish to be controlled they should not be forgiven.

I've seen this in some people you'd least expect it from. It's not uncommon in recovered (or recovering) alcoholics who, having struggled for years, have finally beaten this awful addiction and returned to normal life. Since they have beaten it, they seem to reason, anyone can—if they really want to. Self-righteousness creeps in and impatience increases with those who don't seem to be 'trying hard enough'. It's all very understandable. I think this explains, in part, why it was that Jesus always seemed to be in trouble with the righteous and law-abiding people in the Gospels. These people really *were* decent and upright. They weren't sinless, of course, but they weren't degenerates either and because their behaviour was so different from the bulk of those around them they became 'too hard' and it's a sin to be too hard!

The Bible, and the New Testament scriptures in particular, makes it very clear that forgiveness is not 'easy' for God since He experiences holy recoil from evil. Whatever else the cross of Christ may teach us, the Christian would say, it teaches us that forgiveness is no cheap and easy transaction.

I'm not saying God had to be persuaded by the atoning death of Jesus Christ to forgive us. That would be missing the fact that the death of Christ was God's *gift* to us and that His death was the means by which God worked our forgiveness. No, but however the death of Christ is related to the forgiveness of sins, that is, whatever His death's *precise* connection with our forgiveness is, the New Testament teaches us that His death was *essential* to our forgiveness. And that being true, forgiveness can hardly be seen as cheap or as a routine gift.

Forgiveness is a complex reality. Those who dismiss

injustice and oppression as of no consequence know nothing of forgiveness. To believe there is nothing really to answer for means that 'forgiveness' is redundant. Those who believe that forgiveness is and must be a reality bring in things like: admission of guilt (sins exists and I did do wrong), acceptance of responsibility (I can't place the blame on others), renunciation of the sin (I recognise the evil of what I've done and denounce it), purpose to avoid it in the future (I cannot reject it now but feel it's my right to do it again when it suits me) and a trusting of oneself to the grace of the wounded or dishonoured one (I can't *demand* that they put the offence aside and go on as before).

We must resist the temptation to place all offences on the same level and we must resist the temptation to demand that others place all offences on the same level. Those who can't forgive an occasional act of rudeness without making a major production out of it have a problem of their own to deal with. Those who believe that it's as simple to forgive the torture, rape and murder of a child as it is to forgive a stream of foul language yelled at us by an angry person need to think this whole matter through again. (*This is not to deny that all sins are in need of forgiveness. They are!*)

Because there are so many variables in the lives of people we need to recognise that the creative and gracious act of forgiveness takes on different features in different settings. To equate forgiveness with a brisk, 'It's OK, it's no big deal!' or 'it's all right, it doesn't matter!' misses the point. Forgiveness, if it's real, doesn't support the idea that nothing wrong has happened. A forgiving heart doesn't act as though every unkind act or remark must be dragged out into the open before it is forgiven. Different situations will mean that forgiveness is worked in different ways. To say to a Nazi commandant, 'It's OK, it's no big deal!' is not only to insult all the dishonoured and wounded, it is to violate the sinner and bring self-condemnation on ourselves who should know better.

But however complex the subject, however difficult we find it to forgive those who profess allegiance to Jesus Christ are called to practise forgiveness. And to practise not because it is 'nice' or 'civilised' or 'humane' to forgive, but because God in Christ has forgiven us.

(The Bible plainly teaches that forgiveness and chastisement aren't enemies—they can go hand in hand. It's clearly possible for a person or a group of people to forgive a man for embezzling their money on several occasions, but it may be to the benefit of all concerned (the offender included) if the embezzler is not allowed to handle the money again. To forgive the transgressor is essential, to put the person back in the position of repeated failure might well be cruel and stupid. But these matters call for more discussion than can be offered in this little book.

TWO

My Father isn't like that

I was travelling on a plane from Atlanta to Dallas. There were still a few people on it from a previous leg of the trip and when I got to my seat there was a man sitting there. 'Mister,' I said apologetically, 'I hate to disturb you but this is my seat.' He nodded to the window seat in front of him and said, 'Take that one. The plane's empty.' I told him, 'It is now, but you should see the crowd that's coming on board.' His wife, who was seated on the aisle, said, 'Oh, take that seat.' I patiently explained to her that someone would come and get me out of it saying it was theirs so the move was now or later. A man in the aisle, stretching his legs said, 'There are lots of seats, take that one.' 'Mister,' I responded, 'I'm having trouble enough here, please don't make it harder,' and turning to the man in my seat I pleaded, 'Come on, mister, let me have my seat.' Well, he got really angry, flung his belongings from the middle seat into the aisle, dragged some more from under the seat in front of him and climbed out over his wife into the aisle.

I was red with embarrassment. I climbed over his wife, stuffed my little case under the seat in front of me as she went on and on about the trouble I was creating, telling the people who were coming on how difficult and how thoughtless I was being. Then she said, 'And besides, that's my husband's seat.' I had wanted to suffer in silence but that was too much so I took out my boarding pass with 15A on it and politely but firmly told her, 'No, lady, the seat is mine. See? 15A!' Her next words killed me. '*This isn't 15A!*' she said. I came to life long enough to look up in horror. I was sitting in *16A*. The seat I continued to refuse was mine! The seat I had insisted on getting was his!

Now my chest was hurting, I was sticky with sweat and I said, 'Lady, what can I tell you? I'm *very* sorry.' She snapped back, 'You ought to be!' I dragged out my case and dropped it into the seat in front of me, climbed out over her and sank into my seat like water going down a waste pipe. Humiliated, sick at my stupidity, sweating with shame, my chest hurting and my head throbbing I sat and listened as she told the whole plane about my thoughtlessness, troublemaking and how all along she knew it was her husband's seat. On and on she went about the kind of person I was. I was feeling ill and wanted to turn to her and say, 'Lady, *please*! If you only knew how terrible I feel over the trouble I've caused; if you only knew how you were hurting me by proclaiming my shame to everyone, you'd give me a break and leave me alone.' But I couldn't and she wouldn't turn me loose until she was quite finished.

I want you to know that my Father isn't like that! To those in covenant relationship with Him He promises that he will not remember their wrongs against them so as to destroy the relationship. He is not like a dog which keeps on worrying a bone. I live in a land where we keep a detailed record of wrongs committed by 'the other side' as though we ourselves were free from villainy so it isn't easy to appreciate a God who distinctly remembers forgetting.

And then, to balance things out, some of us have the utmost pleasure of meeting up with people, as I have, who are just like God in this matter. People who with severe mercy deal with the (genuine) wrongs and have done with it—permanently! People from whom you couldn't pry out shame with a crow-bar.

THREE

The sin of being hard

How would this sit with us? 'There, there, you didn't mean to be bad! It's true that for more than ten years you systematically robbed thousands of people of their hard-earned life's savings and you wrote to your friends saying that the 'suckers' seemed eager to part with their money. It's also true that many thousands of older couples have lost their homes and security because of what you've done. But you have no doubt learned from all this and you will behave better in the future. I hereby give you a suspended sentence. I won't revoke your estate-licence because, after all, you have to make a living.' That would be hard! It would be hard on the victims who are owed more than money. The judge's handling of the case adds injustice to injustice and, in some ways, the judge has damaged the people worse than the swindler.

Jesus Christ lived and died to bring forgiveness to criminals but even He wrecked the stalls of profiteers in the temple and denounced the church leaders whose traditions robbed aged parents of the help they should have received from their children. Don't believe anyone, not anyone, who tells you that God isn't concerned about justice. But it's still possible in every-day life to be too hard!

In George Eliot's, *Mill on the Floss*, the heroine is sweet Maggie Tulliver. She loves a crippled boy, Philip Wakem, and he loves her; but it's a doomed relationship, they are not allowed to love one another and they both know it. Still, they speak loving words to one another and that only makes a hopeless situation more difficult. Maggie's brother, Tom, is an upright person but he lacks warmth, compassion and humanity and after he has humiliated Philip and forbidden both he and Maggie to meet again, he turns on his sister. He coldly punishes her again with words that hurt her heart and that's when she says to him: 'I know I've done wrong— often, continually. But yet, sometimes when I have done wrong, it has been because I have feelings that you would be the better for, if you had them. If *you* were in fault ever—if you had done anything very wrong, I should be sorry for the pain it brought you; I should not want punishment heaped on you. But you have always enjoyed punishing me—you have always been hard and cruel to me: even when I was a little girl. I love you better than any one else in the world but you would let me go crying to bed without forgiving me. You have no pity, you have no sense of your own imperfection and your own sins. It is a sin to be hard; it is not fitting for a mortal—for a Christian...'

Coventry Patmore, said J. S. Stewart, sent his disobedient little boy to bed, unkissed and unforgiven, but the father could find no rest. Later he went quietly into the child's room where he lay sleeping, his face still wet with tears; and there on a little table near his head he had gathered some of his favourite toys—a box of counters, a few shells, one or two copper coins—to comfort his sad little heart in his loss. The father gently kissed away the tears and left some of his own and the thought struck him that maybe God felt the same toward all his sons and daughters the way he was feeling toward his own sorrowful and lonely child. He said it in a poem:

When Thou rememberst of what toys
We made our joys,
How weakly understood
Thy great commanded good,
Then fatherly, not less
Than I whom Thou hast moulded
    from the clay,
Thou wilt leave Thy wrath,
    and say,
'I will be sorry for their childishness.'

Every loving mother or father, even though they know better than to 'spoil their child rotten', knows what it is to understand and forgive. And they feel it in their bones that a God as great as the one Jesus Christ revealed to the world has 'motherly' and 'fatherly' ways in him. And we all know that we make allowances for background influences, for peer pressure, fears and personal limitations. And, thank goodness, we think we should. We are not always sure where to draw the line; we're sure that justice matters and that potential victims must be protected, but deep down within us we know there is a sin of being hard.

We insist on avoiding a weak-kneed indulgence (which is the protection of the vulnerable against the cruel and vicious) but we do believe that deep inside the mass of people still lives the little boy or girl who needs to be treated with compassion as well as sternness. We know that there is a sin of being hard!

In a moment, when they don't know you are looking, take a long look at the one who is your companion for life. Or the one you gave life to. Or the one who gave you life and toils for you. Or that brother or sister of yours. Be sure! Be brave, but be sure. There is a sin of being hard.

FOUR

The Scarlet Letter

'Forgiveness' only has meaning for those who confess there is such a thing as 'wrong'. A Christian would speak of 'sin' but if 'wrong' is the best you can do right now, it's where you ought to begin. It isn't enough, but it's a beginning.

There are those who hold themselves to no standard of right behaviour or attitude so they care nothing about not being forgiven. Forgiveness is a subject which has meaning only for the morally sensitive. Does that sound rather pompous? Perhaps, but I believe it's no more than the truth; think about it.

Where the sensitive are wrestling with the wrongs in their lives there is a need for many things but there is an immediate need for forgiveness. The heart that has sinned and can find no forgiveness is utterly scalded and life is agonizing. Though its language is rather dated now, making it a little harder for moderns to enjoy reading it, the most insightful study I know involving the need for forgiveness and the awful results of not getting it, is Nathaniel Hawthorne's novel, *The Scarlet Letter*.

The setting is a Puritan colony in Massachusetts and the two leading characters are Hester Prynne and Arthur

Dimmesdale. Hester had been sent ahead to America by her husband who said he would join her soon, but more than two years passed and she had heard not a word from him or about him. During this time she has been immoral and in due time her shame becomes visible; she gives birth to a child.

After a time in prison she is released but the community punishes her by placing her periodically on a raised platform before the gaze of the whole people. Clergymen would often stop her in the street and deliver sermons on the wickedness of immorality, children would follow her and call her names. In addition she must wear a dress with a large, scarlet letter 'A' embroidered onto it which would proclaim the nature of her crime. They entreat and sometimes bully her to name her partner in crime but she steadfastly refuses to reveal it.

One of the leaders of the community is young Arthur Dimmesdale, a capable and much-loved preacher of truth. There are sermons to be preached against such behaviour and Arthur is instructed by the elders of the community to do this while Hester sits, baby in arms, in the centre of the meeting. Again and again while they are alone Arthur begs her to reveal the name of her fellow-sinner but she won't. It would be easier on her and just, he would tell her; but she wouldn't reveal the name.

What the community did not know but was shared between Arthur and Hester was that *he* was her guilty partner! And Dimmesdale could find no peace. How could he free himself from the crushing truth? He's intelligent— will he ease the pain by burying himself in theological studies? How can he think God's thoughts under these circumstances? He's a capable preacher—will he inspire others to live heroic and pure lives for God? But how can he inspire others to heroism while he himself is daily a coward? He is a servant—will he spend himself, humbly going from door to door to alleviate the loneliness and suffering of the needy and find peace in this way? How can he find peace easing the burdens of others while the love of his life, having faced the wrong she has committed, sees the letter 'A' on her breast as no longer a mark of shame but the name of the one she loves—how can he find peace when she is suffering alone? In the end he joins Hester as an object of public shame.

Dimmesdale's terrible anguish is reflected in the words of a psalmist who said about his own sin, 'When I kept silent my bones wasted away through my groaning all day long. For night and day Your hand was heavy upon me; my strength was sapped as in the heat of summer. Then I acknowledged my sin to You and did not cover up my iniquity. I said, "I will confess my transgressions to the Lord"—and You forgave the guilt of my sin.'

The harsh and relentless, Roger Chillingworth, shrewdly guesses early on who the father is and, knowing the anguish which must exist in the heart of the preacher, asks if the preacher thinks Hester, with her scarlet letter is more miserable than her fellow-criminal. The certain answer is that Arthur is even more miserable than Hester.

The one awful omission in *The Scarlet Letter* is 'forgiveness'. The one thing the heart cried out for and which wasn't dealt with was forgiveness. The young minister publicly confesses and dies in shame without the assurance of forgiveness. He even resists Hester's plea that he predict a reunion in heaven and urges her to remember that they broke the law. This is not the message strugglers need to hear! We mustn't make forgiveness, a cheap passing over of wrongs—'Of course God will forgive you,' said the philosopher Heine, 'that's His business'—but we must leave no struggler in doubt about the fullness and freeness of forgiveness.

We must turn the gaze of the struggler away from his sin once it has been genuinely acknowledged and speak of forgiveness. There must be no self-righteousness involved in the transaction; no impression of pomposity, no patronising of the transgressor. We must join in the joy of heaven when the sinner returns seeking forgiveness and must speak it in the name of God without reservation. Without this there can be no peace for the sensitive and certainly no self-acceptance or self-respect.